THE CELEBRITY BOOK OF SUPER LISTS

Also by Ed Lucaire:

The Celebrity Book of Lists
Celebrity Trivia
*Joan Embery's Collection of Amazing Animal
Facts* (with Joan Embery)

THE CELEBRITY BOOK OF SUPER LISTS

Fantastic Facts About the Famous

Ed Lucaire

STEIN AND DAY/*Publishers*/New York

First published in 1985
Copyright © 1985 by Edward Lucaire
All rights reserved, Stein and Day, Incorporated
Designed by Louis A. Ditizio
Printed in the United States of America
STEIN AND DAY/*Publishers*
Scarborough House
Briarcliff Manor, N.Y. 10510

Library of Congress Cataloging in Publication Data

Lucaire, Ed.
   The celebrity book of super lists.

   Includes index.
   1. United States—Social registers.   2. Fame—
Social aspects—United States. I. Title.
E154.7.L83   1985   920'.009'04   85-40623
ISBN 0-8128-3005-9

to Lewise, Laurin, and Eddie

Acknowledgments

I wish to thank the following people and institutions for their cooperation:

The New York Public Library, the Beaumont (Texas) Public Library, Marketing Evaluations/TVQ, the Friars Club, the Hollywood Historic Trust, the Hasty Pudding Institute of 1770, John Howard, Gary Gold, Alice Lucaire, *Radio & Records* magazine, NBC-TV, Taki, George Cuttingham, Blackglama, Elvira Hess, *People* magazine, Al Goldstein, Benton Arnovitz, Jacques de Spoelberch, Lewise Lucaire, Liz Smith, Kent Laymon, Laurin Lucaire, K. M. Thompson, Jane O'Reilly, Marion Long, Jim Hayden, Madam Tussaud's Wax Museum, Jim Moore, and Rolf Spaeth.

Contents

THE CELEBRITY
BOOK OF
SUPER
LISTS

The Stars Are Born 1.

BORN ON VALENTINE'S DAY

One might suspect that many people are conceived on St. Valentine's Day, but here are some well-known people who were actually delivered on this lovers' holiday:

	DATE OF BIRTH
Mel Allen	February 14, 1913
Jack Benny	February 14, 1894
Carl Bernstein	February 14, 1944
Hugh Downs	February 14, 1921
Stu Erwin	February 14, 1902
Woody Hayes	February 14, 1913
Florence Henderson	February 14, 1934
Gregory Hines	February 14, 1946
Jimmy Hoffa	February 14, 1913
Vic Morrow	February 14, 1932
James Pike	February 14, 1913
Thelma Ritter	February 14, 1905
Paul Tsongas	February 14, 1941
Mickey Wright	February 14, 1935

BORN ON CHRISTMAS DAY

Humphrey Bogart often complained about being born on Christmas because he was "cheated out of birthday presents." Here is a list of notables who also might or might not have agreed with Bogart:

	DATE OF BIRTH
Yehoshua Ben-Yosef	December 25, 4 B.C.*
Humphrey Bogart	December 25, 1899
Cab Calloway	December 25, 1907
Clark M. Clifford	December 25, 1906
Larry Csonka	December 25, 1946
Nellie Fox	December 25, 1927
Sir Lew Grade	December 25, 1906
Conrad Hilton	December 25, 1887
Little Richard	December 25, 1935
Barton MacLane	December 25, 1900
Barbara Mandrell	December 25, 1948
Tony Martin	December 25, 1913
Mike Mazurki	December 25, 1909
Dan Pastorini	December 25, 1949
Robert Leroy Ripley	December 25, 1893
Kyle Rote, Jr.	December 25, 1950
Anwar el-Sadat	December 25, 1918
Rod Serling	December 25, 1924
Moses Soyer	December 25, 1899
Raphael Soyer	December 25, 1899
Sissy Spacek	December 25, 1949
Phil Spector	December 25, 1940
Ken Stabler	December 25, 1945
Helen Twelvetrees	December 25, 1908
Maurice Utrillo	December 25, 1883
Lila Acheson Wallace	December 25, 1889

---

*Strange as it seems, Biblical scholars calculate that the birth of the man who has come to be known as Jesus Christ actually occurred four years earlier than the date originally calculated by the monk Dionysius Exiguus in the 6th century after Christ.

CELEBRITIES BORN ON
EXACTLY THE SAME DAY*

	DATE OF BIRTH
Barry Goldwater and Dana Andrews	January 1, 1909
Joan Baez and Susannah York	January 9, 1941
Patsy Kelly and Luise Rainer	January 12, 1910
Eartha Kitt and Roger Vadim	January 26, 1928
Vanessa Redgrave and Boris Spassky	January 30, 1937
Carol Channing, Joanne Dru, and Norman Mailer	January 31, 1923
Eva Gabor, Kim Stanley, and Virginia E. Johnson	February 11, 1925
Brian Bedford and Sonny Bono	February 16, 1935
Bill Cullen and Jack Palance	February 18, 1920
James T. Farrell and Peter DeVries	February 27, 1910
Mickey Spillane and George Lincoln Rockwell	March 9, 1918
Rudolf Nureyev and Monique Van Vooren	March 17, 1938
Larry Elgart, Carl Reiner, and Ray Goulding	March 20, 1922
Herb Alpert and Richard Chamberlain	March 31, 1935
Marlon Brando and Doris Day	April 3, 1924
Marsha Mason and Wayne Newton	April 3, 1942
Chester Bowles and Melvyn Douglas	April 5, 1901
Loretta Lynn and Tony Perkins	April 14, 1932
Roy Clark and Elizabeth Montgomery	April 15, 1933
Lindsay Anderson and Henry Mancini	April 16, 1923
Corinne Calvet and Cloris Leachman	April 30, 1926
Peter Benchley and Ricky Nelson	May 8, 1940
Albert Finney and Glenda Jackson	May 9, 1936
Yogi Berra and John Simon	May 12, 1925
Peter Shaffer and Anthony Shaffer	May 15, 1926
Raymond Burr and Dennis Day	May 21, 1917
Richard Benjamin and Susan Strasberg	May 22, 1938
Marilyn Monroe and Andy Griffith	June 1, 1926
Colleen Dewhurst and Allen Ginsberg	June 3, 1926
Marisa Pavan and Pier Angeli	June 19, 1932
Chet Atkins and Audie Murphy	June 20, 1924
Gower Champion and Joseph Papp	June 22, 1921

---

*See preceding separate Valentine's Day and Christmas lists.

CELEBRITIES BORN ON EXACTLY THE SAME DAY,
continued

	DATE OF BIRTH
Alfred Kinsey and the Duke of Windsor	June 23, 1894
Lena Horne and Buddy Rich	June 30, 1917
Karen Black and Genevieve Bujold	July 1, 1942
Stephen Boyd and Gina Lollobrigida	July 4, 1928
Ingmar Bergman and Arthur Laurents	July 14, 1918
Diana Rigg and Natalie Wood	July 20, 1938
Ernest Hemingway and Hart Crane	July 21, 1899
Blake Edwards and Jason Robards, Jr.	July 26, 1922
Clara Bow and Thelma Todd	July 29, 1905
Lionel Bart and Geoffrey Holder	August 1, 1930
Carroll O'Connor and James Baldwin	August 2, 1924
Jimmy Dean and Eddie Fisher	August 10, 1928
Buddy Greco and Alice Ghostley	August 14, 1926
Julia Child and Wendy Hiller	August 15, 1912
Denton Cooley and Ray Bradbury	August 22, 1920
Yvonne DeCarlo and Vittorio Gassman	September 1, 1922
Martha Mitchell and Allen Drury	September 2, 1918
Denise Darcel and Peter Sellers	September 8, 1925
Greta Garbo and Eddie Anderson	September 18, 1905
Duke Snider and Lurleen Wallace	September 19, 1926
Laurence Harvey and George Peppard	October 1, 1928
Bud Abbott and Groucho Marx	October 2, 1895
Sarah Churchill and Alfred Drake	October 7, 1914
Cornel Wilde and Jack MacGowran	October 13, 1918
Vivien Leigh and John McGiver	November 5, 1913
Brian Keith and Johnny Desmond	November 14, 1921
W. Averell Harriman and Field Marshal Erwin Rommel	November 15, 1891
Woody Allen and Lou Rawls	December 1, 1935
Jean-Luc Godard and Andy Williams	December 3, 1930
Broderick Crawford and Lee J. Cobb	December 9, 1911
Lillian Roth and Van Heflin	December 13, 1910
Abbe Lane and Lee Remick	December 14, 1935
Ava Gardner and Leadbelly	December 24, 1922
John Denver and Sarah Miles	December 31, 1943

So much for astrology!

BORN IN BABYLON ... HOLLYWOOD THAT IS

In his haunting book *Hollywood Babylon,* writer and ex-actor Kenneth Anger told many sordid tales of luminaries whose lights were extinguished within jogging distance of Sunset Boulevard. The following people were *born* in Babylon:

Lucie Arnaz	Jack Jones
Diane Baker	John Philip Law
Beau Bridges	Yvette Mimieux
Kim Carnes	Elizabeth Montgomery
David Carradine	Don Murray
Tina Cole	Jay North
Kim Darby	Bud Palmer
John Derek	Stefanie Powers
Terri Garr	Katharine Ross
Leif Garrett	Dean Stockwell
Dan Haggerty	Michael Tilson Thomas
Jerome Hines	

CELEBRITY BROOKLYNITES

The Celebrity Book of Lists (Stein and Day), listed dozens of well-known people who were born in Brooklyn, from the expected (comedians like Buddy Hackett, Gabe Kaplan, Alan King, and Joan Rivers and singers like Vic Damone, Neil Diamond, Steve Lawrence) to the unexpected (Mary Tyler Moore, Marion Davies, Emil Jannings). But lots more Brooklyn-born celebrities have been unearthed, and here they are:

Pat Benatar	Arlo Guthrie
Helen Boehm	Elizabeth Janeway
James Brady	Abraham Maslow
Hugh Carey	Stephanie Mills
Gerry Cooney	Eddie Money
Aaron Copland	Eddie Murphy
J. P. Donleavy	Priscilla Presley
Lou Ferrigno	Eddie Rabbit
Milton Friedman	Constance Talmadge
Vitas Gerulitis	Wolfman Jack
Bob Guccione	

SINGERS FROM PHILADELPHIA

Comedians come from Brooklyn and singers come from Philadelphia—it's a show business lesson in geography. Here are some well-known singers from Philadelphia and their real names:

Frankie Avalon (Francis Avalonne)
Chubby Checker (Ernest Evans)
Jim Croce
James Darren (James Ercolani)
Fabian (Fabian Forte)
Eddie Fisher (Edwin Fisher)
Buddy Greco
Bill Haley
Mario Lanza (Alfred Arnold Cocozza)
Al Martino
Bobby Rydell (Robert Riderelli)

BORN IN TEXAS

Texas is one of the United States, but the cliche is true; it is also a state of mind. Few Texans are ambivalent about their heritage. They have about ten times more *esprit de corps* per capita than, say, people from Rhode Island,* and a much greater capacity for chili. The following stars are Lone Stars but they're not alone:

Alvin Ailey	Mac Davis	Waylon Jennings
Debbie Allen	Jimmy Dean	Carolyn Jones
Gene Autry	Sandy Duncan	Evelyn Keyes
Jo Don Baker	Shelley Duvall	Kris Kristofferson
Robby Benson	Dale Evans	Josh Logan
Carol Burnett	Morgan Fairchild	Trini Lopez
Gary Busey	Farrah Fawcett	Bessie Love
Vikki Carr	Kathryn Grant	Barbara Mandrell
Cyd Charisse	Larry Hagman	Mary Martin
Kathryn Crosby	Ann Harding	Steve Martin
Christopher Cross	Martha Hyer	Curt Massey

*The area of Texas, by the way, is 216 times larger than that of Rhode Island.

Tex McCrary
Spanky McFarland
Ann Miller
Willie Nelson
James Noble
Buck Owens
Fess Parker
Valerie Perrine
Paula Prentiss
Ray Price
Rex Reed

Debbie Reynolds
Johnny Rodriquez
Kenny Rogers
Boz Scaggs
Lori Singer
Jaclyn Smith
Liz Smith
Sissy Spacek
Stephen Stills
Gale Storm

B.J. Thomas
Rip Torn
Tanya Tucker
Tommy Tune
Tina Turner
King Vidor
Helen Vinson
Barry White
Mason Williams
Chill Wills

CELEBRITIES BORN IN NEBRASKA

Nebraska, for a state with a small population, grows a lot more than corn and wheat: it also grows talent. Here are the names of some celebrities who were born in the Cornhusker State:

John Archer
Adele Astaire
Fred Astaire
Max Baer
Bil Baird
Marlon Brando
Dick Cavett
Montgomery Clift
James Coburn
Sandy Dennis
Henry Fonda
Gerald R. Ford

Hoot Gibson
Leland Hayward
Neal Hefti
David Janssen
Melvin Laird
Harold Lloyd
Dorothy McGuire
Fred Niblo
Patricia Ryan Nixon
Nick Nolte
Elmo Roper, Jr.

Ted Sorensen
Skip Stephenson
Robert Taylor
Paul Williams
Roger Williams
Julie Wilson
Don Wilson
Irene Worth
Malcolm X
Sam Yorty
Darryl Zanuck

Note: Johnny Carson was born in Corning, Iowa.

BORN IN RUSSIA AND THE USSR

The man* who wrote the songs "White Christmas" and "Easter Parade" was one of those born in Russia:

Boris Aronson	Vladimir Horowitz	Maria Ouspenskaya
Mischa Auer	Ida Kaminska	Ayn Rand
George Balanchine	Andre Kostelanetz	Gregory Ratoff
Mikhail Baryshnikov	Meyer Lansky	Mark Rothko
Irving Berlin*	Eugenie Leontovich	David Rubinoff
Yul Brynner	Max Lerner	George Sanders
Marc Chagall	Sam Levene	David Sarnoff
Tom Conway	Natalia Makarova	Moses Soyer
Alexandria Danilova	Leonide Massine	Ralphael Soyer
Ariel Durant	Golda Meir	Isaac Stern
Igor Gorin	Lewis Milestone	Akim Tamiroff
Sir Lew Grade	Nathan Milstein	Sophie Tucker
Philippe Halsman	Rudolf Nureyev	Efrem Zimbalist
Jascha Heifetz		

FAMOUS PEOPLE BORN IN POLAND

Polly Adler	Pola Negri
Sholem Asch	Shimon Peres
Menachem Begin	Pope John Paul II
David Ben-Gurion	Hyman G. Rickover
Jacob Bronowski	Leo Rosten
Zbigniew Brzezinski	Artur Rubinstein
Myron Cohen	Helena Rubenstein
Bella Darvi	Elisabeth Schwarzkopf
David Dubinsky	Isaac Bashevis Singer
Max Factor	Menasha Skulnik
Samuel Goldwyn	Andrzej Wajda
Jerzy Kosinski	Harry Warner
Bronislaw Malinowski	Simon Wiesenthal
Ross Martin	

CELEBRITY EXPATRIATES

Josephine Baker—Born in St. Louis, Missouri, in 1906, this singer became a French citizen in 1937.

T. S. Eliot—Also born in St. Louis, but in 1888, this poet and playwright later became a British subject in 1927.

John Huston—This writer and movie director was also born in Missouri (Nevada, Missouri). He became a citizen of Ireland in 1964, having maintained residence there since the 1930s.

Lee Harvey Oswald—The assassin of John F. Kennedy was born in New Orleans, Louisiana. He renounced his U.S. citizenship in 1959 and applied for Soviet citizenship when he lived in that country.

Elizabeth Taylor—Miss Taylor was born in London, England, of American parents and therefore had dual citizenship. However, when she married Richard Burton in 1964, she became a British subject.

Family Matters | 2.

FAMOUS RELATIVES

Film actress **Lauren Bacall,** whose real name is Betty Perske, is a first cousin of Israel's Prime Minister **Shimon Peres,** who was born Shimon Perske.

Actor and raconteur **Orson Bean** is a third cousin of Calvin Coolidge, 30th president of the United States.

Singer **Pat Boone** is a descendant of pioneer Daniel Boone, as is oil magnate T. Boone Pickens.

Actor **Bruce Dern's** grandfather, George H. Dern, was Secretary of War during one of Franklin D. Roosevelt's administrations and was also governor of Utah. Dern is also great-nephew of poet Archibald MacLeish.

Singer **Nelson Eddy** was a descendant of Martin Van Buren, the eighth U.S. president. Actor **Glenn Ford** is also a descendant of Van Buren.

And speaking of pioneers, **Peter Fonda's** second wife, Portia, is a great-great-great-granddaughter of Davy Crockett.

Choreographer **Martha Graham** is a descendant of Captain Miles Standish, the English settler and *Mayflower* passenger.

Actress **Mariette Hartley's** maternal grandfather was behavioral psychologist John B. Watson.

The late newscaster **Chet Huntley** was a descendant of John Adams and John Quincy Adams.

Former baseball commissioner **Bowie Kuhn,** received his unusual first name because he is a descendant of defender of the Alamo, Jim Bowie, after whom the Bowie knife was named.

Actor **Burt Lancaster** traces his ancestry back to the royal English House of Lancaster.

FAMOUS RELATIVES, continued

Sophia Loren's sister Maria married Romano Mussolini, the son of Italian dictator Benito Mussolini.

TV commentator **Roger Mudd** is a descendant of Dr. Samuel Mudd, the Maryland doctor who gave medical assistance to John Wilkes Booth, the man who assassinated Abraham Lincoln. Playwright **William Inge** was a distant relative of Edwin and John Wilkes Booth.

The maternal grandfather of singer **Olivia Newton-John** was Nobel Prize-winning German-Jewish physicist Max Born.

Richard M. Nixon is a descendant of King Edward III of England.

MacLean Stevenson's paternal great-uncle Adlai E. Stevenson was Grover Cleveland's vice-president (second administration) and a cousin of the late Illinois governor and presidential candidate of the same name.

FAMOUS IN-LAWS

Fame is a relative thing. Here are some well-known people who are in-laws of other well-known people:

	PARENT(S)-IN-LAW
Peter Lawford	Dan Rowan
Rick Nelson	Tom Harmon
Denny McLain	Louis Boudreau
Pat Boone	Red Foley
Debby Boone	Rosemary Clooney/José Ferrer
Frank Sinatra	Maureen O'Sullivan/John Farrow
Artie Shaw	Jerome Kern
Anthony Quinn	Cecil B. de Mille
Robert Walker	John Ford
Oskar Werner	Tyrone Power
Tom Hayden	Henry Fonda
Tommy Sands	Frank Sinatra
Geraldo Rivera	Kurt Vonnegut, Jr.
Robert Walker	Ward Bond

W. H. Auden	Thomas Mann
Sidney Lumet	Lena Horne
Tom Ewell	George Abbott
Jason Miller	Jackie Gleason
David O. Selznick	Louis B. Mayer
Jacob Javits	Alfred T. Ringling
Dorothy Hamill	Dean Martin
Burt Lancaster	Ernie Kovacs
Sandy Koufax	Richard Widmark

FAMOUS MEN WHO BECAME
FATHERS AT A LATE AGE

Most men father their last child, if any child at all, in their 30s. Here are some well-known men who became fathers relatively late:

	AGE
Andres Segovia	76
Charlie Chaplin	73
Strom Thurmond	69*
Cary Grant	62
Clark Gable	61*
Ronald Colman	53*
Roger Corman	49
Humphrey Bogart	49
Bertrand Russell	49*
Mark Rothko	47*

*First or only child

FAMOUS WOMEN WHO HAD BABIES
AT A LATE AGE

	AGE	YEAR
Gloria Vanderbilt	44	1968
Ursula Andress	44	1980
Martha Mitchell	43	1961
Rose Kennedy	42	1932
Lucille Ball	42	1953
Svetlana Stalin	42	1971
Alice Roosevelt Longworth	41	1925
Happy Rockefeller	41	1967
Audrey Hepburn	41	1970
Rosalynn Carter	40	1967
Claudia Cardinale	40	1979
Diana Rigg	39	1977
Sophia Loren	38	1971
Helena Rubenstein	38	1909
Yoko Ono	37	1975
Jean Shrimpton	37	1979

MAIDEN NAMES OF CELEBRITIES' MOTHERS

Allen, Steve
  Isabel Donahue
  (a.k.a. Belle Montrose)
Annenberg, Walter
  Sadie Cecilia Friedman
Attenborough, Richard
  Mary Clegg
Bacall, Lauren
  Natalie Weinstein
Bacharach, Burt
  Irma Freeman
Baker, Russell
  Lucy Elizabeth Robinson
Bennett, Michael
  Helen Turnoff
Black, Shirley Temple
  Gertrude Creiger
Bradbury, Ray
  Esther Marie Moberg

Bradley, Sen. Bill
  Susan Crowe
Brokaw, Tom
  Eugenia Conley
Brooks, Louise
  Myra Rude
Buckley, William F., Jr.
  Aloise Steiner
Bush, George
  Dorothy Walker
Carson, Johnny
  Ruth Hook
Carter, Hodding III
  Betty Werlein
Carter, Jimmy
  Lillian Gordy
Cavett, Dick
  Eva Richards

Cohen, Sen. William S.
  Clara Hartley
Collins, Joan
  Elsa Bessant
Dale, Jim
  Miriam Wells
de Kooning, William
  Cornelia Nobel
Davis, Mac
  Edith Irene Lankford
Di Palma, Brian
  Vivenne Muti
Donahue, Phil
  Catherine McClory
Ellington, Duke
  Daisy Kennedy
Fellini, Federico
  Ida Barbiani
Ferraro, Geraldine
  Antonetta L. Corrieri
Forman, Milos
  Anna Svabova
Foster, Jodie
  Evelyn Almond
Friedan, Betty
  Miriam Horwitz
Gibb, Barry
  Barbara Pass
Gibson, Mel
  Eva Mylott
Ginsberg, Allen
  Naomi Levy
Guinness, Alec
  Agnes Guff
Guthrie, Arlo
  Marjorie Mazia Greenblatt
Hart, Kitty Carlisle
  Hortense Holzman
Hartman, David
  Fannie Redman Downs

Hirsch, Judd
  Sally Kitzis
Hoffman, Dustin
  Florence Schanberg
Hopkins, Anthony
  Muriel Anne Yeats
Houseman, John
  May Davies
Huston, John
  Reah Gore
Iacocca, Lee
  Antoinette Perrotto
Iglesias, Julio
  Maria del Rosario de la Cueva
  Perignat
Jackson, Anne
  Stella Germain Murray
Jackson, Michael
  Katherine Esther Scruse
Jacobi, Derek
  Daisy Gertrude Masters
Jennings, Peter
  Elizabeth Ewart Osborne
King, Alan
  Minnie Solomon
King, Stephen
  Nellie Ruth Pillsbury
Krantz, Judith
  Mary Braeger
Kuralt, Charles
  Ina Bishop
Liddy, G. Gordon
  Maria Abba Ticchio
Ludlum, Robert
  Margaret Wadsworth
Mailer, Norman
  Fanny Schneider
Mandrell, Barbara
  Mary Ellen McGill

Mangione, Chuck
Nancy Bellavia
Mason, Marsha
Jacqueline Rakowski
McKellen, Ian
Margery Sutcliffe
McMurtry, Larry
Hazel Ruth McIver
Miller, Ann
Clara Birdwell
Miller, Jonathan
Betty Bergson Spiro
Milnes, Sherrill
Thelma Roe
Moore, Dudley
Ada Francis Hughes
Moore, Mary Tyler
Marjorie Hackett
Mudd, Roger
Irma Iris Harrison
Murray, Anne
Marion Burke
Nelligan, Kate
Alice Dier
Orbach, Jerry
Emily O'Lexy
Pakula, Alan J.
Jeannette Goldstein
Paterno, Joe
Florence de Salle
Peters, Bernadette
Marguerite Maltese
Porter, Sylvia
Rose Maisel
Prince, Harold
Blanche Stern
Reagan, Nancy
Edith Luckett
Redford, Robert
Martha Hart

Ritter, John
Dorothy Fay Southworth
Rivera, Chita
Katherine Anderson
Rogers, Kenny
Lucille Hester
Rogers, Fred "Mr."
Nancy McFeeley
Rogers, Roy
Mattie Martha Womack
Rooney, Andy
Ellinor Reynolds
Roth, Philip
Bess Finkel
Safer, Morley
Anna Cohn
Sagan, Carl
Rachel Molly Gruber
Segal, Erich
Cynthia Shapiro
Sharif, Omar
Claire Saada
Sidney, Sylvia
Rebecca Saperstein
Sills, Beverly
Shirley Bahn
Stockman, David
Carol Bartz
Sutherland, Donald
Dorothy Isabel McNichol
Tandy, Jessica
Jessie Helen Horspool
Torme, Mel
Sarah "Betty" Sopkin
Tune, Tommy
Eva Mae Clark
Updike, John
Linda Grace Hoyer
Vaughan, Sarah
Ada Baylor

Vidal, Gore
  Nina Gore
Vonnegut, Kurt Jr.
  Edith Sophia Lieber
Welch, Raquel
  Josephine Hall
Wilder, Billy
  Eugenia Baldinger

Williams, Paul
  Bertha Mae Burnside
Wolfe, Tom
  Helen Perkins Hughes
Wyeth, Andrew
  Carolyn Brenneman Bockius

OCCUPATIONS OF CELEBRITIES' MOTHERS

Bacharach, Burt
  portrait painter
Bennett, Michael
  secretary
Cleaver, Eldridge
  school teacher
Dale, Jim
  shoe factory worker
Dee, Ruby
  school teacher
Deighton, Len
  hotel cook
de Kooning, William
  bartender
Donahue, Phil
  shoe store clerk
Duncan, Sandy
  painter
Fierstein, Harvey
  school librarian
Gibb, Barry
  singer
Gibson, Mel
  opera singer
Guthrie, Arlo
  dance teacher

Hawn, Goldie
  jewelry wholesaler
Hill, Jennifer
  school teacher; seamstress
Huston, John
  journalist
Jackson, Jesse
  maid in a hospital
Jackson, Michael
  Sears Roebuck employee
Kingsley, Ben
  fashion model, actress
Krantz, Judith
  lawyer
Lendl, Ivan
  secretary
Letterman, David
  church secretary
Loudon, Dorothy
  pianist
Mandrell, Barbara
  music teacher
McKuen, Rod
  waitress, telephone operator,
  dance-hall hostess

OCCUPATIONS OF CELEBRITIES' MOTHERS, continued

Miller, Jonathan
  writer
Montana, Joe
  secretary
Murphy, Eddie
  telephone operator
Murray, Anne
  nurse
Rawls, Lou
  talent agent
Reagan, Nancy
  actress
Reeve, Christopher
  newspaper writer
Richie, Lionel
  school principal
Ritter, John
  actress
Rivera, Chita
  government clerk
Schlesinger, John
  violinist
Strawberry, Darryl
  telephone company circuit
  designer

Streep, Meryl
  commercial artist
Sutherland, Donald
  math teacher
Tandy, Jessica
  teacher, clerk
Tormé, Mel
  pianist
Townshend, Peter
  singer
Tubb, Ernest
  pianist, organist
Vadim, Roger
  photographer
Wambaugh, Joseph
  domestic
Williams, Vanessa
  singing teacher
Williams, Billy Dee
  opera singer, elevator operator
Winfield, Dave
  audio-visual aid worker at a
  public school
Winger, Debra
  office manager

FAMOUS CHILDREN OF DOCTORS

W. H. Auden
Barbi Benton (gynecologist)
Jacqueline Bisset
Jean-Luc Godard
Eric Heiden
Katharine Hepburn (urologist)
Julio Iglesias (gynecologist)
Ben Kingsley
Marilyn McCoo

Anne Murray
Randy Newman
Sylvia Porter
Renee Richards
Joan Rivers
Jane Seymour (gynecologist)
Robert Shaw
Sally Struthers

FAMOUS CHILDREN OF DENTISTS

It has been said that dentists are always looking for new professions and so are their children. Here are some well-known people who were not bitten by the desire to pursue the same career as their fathers:

Walter Cronkite
Miles Davis
Robert Evans
Ramon Novarro
Jaclyn Smith
Andrew Young

WELL-KNOWN PEOPLE OF AMERICAN INDIAN DESCENT

Johnny Cash (one-fourth Cherokee)
Cher (part Cherokee)
Redd Foxx (one-fourth Seminole)
James Garner (part Cherokee)
Jimi Hendrix (part Cherokee)
Lena Horne (one-eighth Blackfoot)
Waylon Jennings (part Cherokee and Comanche)
Joe Montana (one-sixty-fourth Sioux)
Robert Rauschenberg (one-fourth Cherokee)
Johnnie Ray (part Blackfoot)
Burt Reynolds (one-fourth Cherokee)
Oral Roberts (part Cherokee)
Roy Rogers (part Choctaw)
Will Rogers (part Cherokee)
Willie Stargell (part Seminole)
Ernest Tubb (one-eighth Cherokee)
Tommy Tune (part Shawnee)
Fernando Valenzuela (part Mayo)

BRIEF ENCOUNTERS: SHORT MARRIAGES

"It takes two to make marriage a success and only one a failure."

—*Herbert Samuel*

COUPLE	LENGTH OF MARRIAGE
Dennis and Karen Lamm	7 months
Burt Lancaster and June Ernst	1 month
Ethel Merman and Ernest Borgnine	3 weeks
Germaine Greer and Paul De Feu	3 weeks
Katharine Hepburn and Ludlow Ogden Smith	3 weeks
Gloria Swanson and Wallace Beery	3 weeks
Patty Duke Astin and Michael Tell	13 days
Dennis Hopper and Michelle Phillips	8 days
Buck Owens and Jana Grief	2 days
Rudolph Valentino and Jean Acker	1 day

FAMOUS UNWED PARENTS

Once an insult, the word meaning "child of unwed parents" is rarely used these days in its precise sense and will probably be removed from most dictionaries. Approximately one out of every five births in the United States is out of wedlock, and the blessings of children conceived in this fashion are not unknown to the world of celebritydom. Here are some couples who have had children but who haven't had the time or the inclination to take out a marriage license:

Vanessa Redgrave and Franco Nero
Grace Slick and Paul Kantner
David Carradine and Barbara Hershey
Lainie Kazan and Peter Daniels
Liv Ullmann and Ingmar Bergman
Mick Jagger and Jeri Hall
Jessica Lange and Mikhail Baryshnikov
Catherine Deneuve and Roger Vadim
Christopher Reeve and Gae Exton
LeVar Burton and Pamela Smith
Farrah Fawcett and Ryan O'Neal
Hayley Mills and Leigh Dawson
Steven Spielberg and Amy Irving
Ursula Andress and Harry Hamlin

CELEBRITY PARENTS OF TWINS

Edward Asner
Alan Bates
Meredith Baxter-Birney
Ingrid Bergman
Debby Boone
Jim Brown
Bing Crosby
Jacques D'Amboise
Donald Dell
Mia Farrow
Milos Forman
Andy Gibb

Mel Gibson
Gunter Grass
Susan Hayward
Loretta Lynn
Henry Mancini
Ricky Nelson
Otto Preminger
Jane Pauley
Nelson Rockefeller
Eric Severeid
James Stewart
Margaret Thatcher

FAMOUS ADOPTED PEOPLE

Edward Albee
Art Buchwald
Deborah Harry
Steven P. Jobs (co-founder of
    Apple Computer)
Art Linkletter
James MacArthur
James Michener

(AND WHERE YOU CAN FIND THEM)

CELEBRITY ADDRESSES

Got a beef? Write a letter! Want to congratulate celebrities on their latest performance, book, article, speech, etc.? Write a nice letter! Here are some addresses of well-known people.

Cindy Adams (columnist)
1050 Fifth Ave.
New York, NY 10028

Don Adams (comedian)
c/o David Licht
9171 Wilshire Blvd.
Beverly Hills, CA 90210

Charles Addams (cartoonist)
c/o *The New Yorker*
25 W. 43rd St.
New York, NY 10036

Edward Albee (playwright)
14 Harrison St.
New York, NY 10013

Eddie Albert (actor)
c/o ICM
8899 Beverly Blvd.
Los Angeles, CA 90048

Alan Alda (actor)
c/o Martin Bregman
    Productions
100 Universal City Plaza
Universal City, CA 91608

Jane Alexander (actress)
Route 2
Gordon Road
Carmel, NY 10512

Peter Allen (singer,
songwriter)
9665 Wilshire Blvd.
Suite 200
Los Angeles, CA 90212

Steve Allen (humorist,
songwriter)
15201 Burbank Blvd.
Van Nuys, CA 91401

Woody Allen (director, writer,
actor)
930 Fifth Ave.
New York, NY 10021

Cleveland Amory (author,
critic)
140 W. 57th St.
New York, NY 10019

CELEBRITY ADDRESSES, continued

Jack Anderson (columnist)
1401 16th St. NW
Washington, D.C. 20036

Julie Andrews (actress)
P.O. Box 666
Beverly Hills, CA 90213

Paul Anka (singer, songwriter)
Box 100
Carmel, CA 93921

Ann-Margret (actress)
9665 Wilshire Blvd.
Suite 200
Beverly Hills, CA 90212

Yassir Arafat (PLO leader)
Palais Essaada La Marsa
Tunis, Tunisia

James Arness (actor)
Box 10480
Glendale, CA 91209

Ashford and Simpson (singers,
songwriters)
c/o G. Sciffer
1155 N. La Cienega Blvd.
Los Angeles, CA 90069

Ed Asner (actor)
4348 Van Nuys Blvd.
Suite 207
Sherman Oaks, CA 91403

Fred Astaire (dancer, actor)
c/o I.C.M.
8899 Beverly Blvd.
Los Angeles, CA 90048

Mary Astor (actress)
Motion Picture Country
Home
23450 Calabasas Rd.
Woodland Hills, CA 91302

Gene Autry (cowboy actor,
singer, and entrepreneur)
Golden West Broadcasting
5858 W. Sunset Blvd.
Hollywood, CA 90028

Richard Avedon
(photographer)
407 E. 75th St.
New York, NY 10021

Hoyt Axton (singer,
songwriter)
P.O. Box 614
Tahoe City, CA 95730

Dan Aykroyd (comic actor)
c/o Atlantic Records
75 Rockefeller Plaza
New York, NY 10019

Charles Aznavour (singer,
actor)
4 Avenue de Lieulee
78 Galluis, France

Lauren Bacall (actress)
c/o S.T.E. Reps. Ltd.
1776 Broadway
New York, NY 10019

James Bacon (columnist)
Los Angeles Herald Examiner
1111 S. Broadway
Los Angeles, CA 90051

James Baldwin (author)
c/o Edward J. Acton
17 Grove St.
New York, NY 10014

Brigitte Bardot (actress)
La Madrique
St. Tropez, France

Rona Barrett (columnist)
P.O. Box 1410
Beverly Hills, CA 90213

Warren Beatty (actor,
director)
J.R.S. Productions
5451 Marathon St.
Hollywood, CA 90038

Harry Belafonte (singer,
actor)
Belafonte Enterprises Inc.
157 W. 57th St.
New York, NY 10019

Michael Bennett
(choreographer, director)
890 Broadway
New York, NY 10003

Tony Bennett (singer)
Agency for Performing Arts
120 W. 57th St.
New York, NY 10019

Candice Bergen (actress)
C.M.A.
8899 Beverly Blvd.
Hollywood, CA 90048

Ingmar Bergman (director)
620 36 Faro
Stockholm, Sweden

Leonard Bernstein (conductor,
composer)
1414 Avenue of the Americas
New York, NY 10019

Yogi Berra (baseball manager)
Sutherland Road
Montclair, NJ 07042

Stephen Birmingham (author)
c/o Brandt and Brandt
1501 Broadway
New York, NY 10036

Jacqueline Bissett (actress)
I.C.M.
8899 Beverly Blvd.
Los Angeles, CA 90048

Erma Bombeck (columnist)
Field Newspaper Syndicate
1703 Kaiser Ave.
Irvine, CA 92714

Pat Boone (singer)
I.C.M.
8899 Beverly Blvd.
Los Angeles, CA 90048

Timothy Bottoms (actor)
c/o Robert Raison Associates
9575 Lime Orchard Rd.
Beverly Hills, CA 90210

David Bowie (singer, actor)
9665 Wilshire Blvd.
Suite 200
Beverly Hills, CA 90212

Ed Bradley (newscaster)
CBS News
524 W. 57th St.
New York, NY 10019

37

Marlon Brando (actor)
Tetiaroa Island
Tahiti

David Brenner (comedian)
c/o William Morris Agency
1350 Avenue of the Americas
New York, NY 10019

Christie Brinkley (model)
151 El Camino
Beverly Hills, CA 90212

David Brinkley (newscaster)
ABC News
1330 Avenue of the Americas
New York, NY 10019

Tom Brokaw (newscaster)
NBC News
30 Rockefeller Plaza
New York, NY 10020

Charles Bronson (actor)
9169 Sunset Blvd.
Los Angeles, CA 90069

Mel Brooks (writer, actor, director)
P.O. Box 900
Beverly Hills, CA 90213

Helen Gurley Brown (editor, author)
1 W. 81st St.
New York, NY 10024

Art Buchwald (columnist)
1750 Pennsylvania Ave. NW
Washington, D.C. 20006

William F. Buckley, Jr. (editor, author)
150 E. 35th St.
New York, NY 10016

Carol Burnett (comedienne, actress)
141 El Camino Drive
Suite 110
Beverly Hills, CA 90212

George Burns (comedian)
1040 N. Las Palmas
Hollywood, CA 90038

James Cagney (actor)
P.O. Box 287
Stanfordville, NY 12581

Dyan Cannon (actress)
1888 Century Park East
Suite 1400
Los Angeles, CA 90067

Princess Caroline (socialite)
Grimaldi Palace
Monte Carlo, Monaco

Johnny Carson (TV talk show host)
3000 W. Alameda
Burbank, CA 91523

Lynda Carter (actress)
P.O. Box 5973
Sherman Oaks, CA 91413

Barbara Cartland (author)
Camfield Place, Hatfield
Hertfordshire, England

Johnny Cash (singer)
711 Summerfield Dr.
Hendersonville, TN 37075

Fidel Castro (Cuban leader)
Palacio del Gobienro
Havana, Cuba

Richard Chamberlain (actor)
1888 Century Park East
Suite 1400
Los Angeles, CA 90067

John Chancellor (newscaster)
NBC News
30 Rockefeller Plaza
New York, NY 10020

Stockard Channing (actress)
151 El Camino
Beverly Hills, CA 90212

Prince Charles (British
royalty)
Kensington Palace
London, W8, England

Chevy Chase (comedic actor)
8966 Sunset Blvd.
Los Angeles, CA 90069

Cher (singer, actress)
c/o Press Office Ltd.
555 Madison Ave.
New York, NY 10022

Dick Clark (producer)
3003 W. Olive Ave.
Burbank, CA 91505

Jill Clayburgh (actress)
c/o William Morris Agency
1350 Avenue of the Americas
New York, NY 10019

James Coburn (actor)
409 N. Camden Dr.
Suite 105
Beverly Hills, CA 90210

Roy Cohn (lawyer)
39 East 68th St.
New York, NY 10021

Gary Coleman (actor)
261 S. Robertson Blvd.
Beverly Hills, CA 90211

Jackie Collins (author)
Simon & Schuster
1230 Avenue of the Americas
New York, NY 10020

Joan Collins (actress)
151 El Camino
Beverly Hills, CA 90212

Jimmy Connors (tennis player)
Gerald Lane
Belleville, IL 60507

Alistair Cooke (TV host)
Nassau Point
Cutchogue, NY 11935

Francis Ford Coppola
(director)
915 Kearny St.
San Francisco, CA 94133

Bill Cosby (comedic actor)
1900 Avenue of the Stars
Suite 1900
Century City, CA 90067

Jamie Lee Curtis (actress)
8642 Melrose Ave.
Suite 200
Los Angeles, CA 90069

Tony Curtis (actor)
P.O. Box 540
Beverly Hills, CA 90213

Sammy Davis, Jr. (entertainer)
151 El Camino
Beverly Hills, CA 90212

Doris Day (actress, singer)
Box 223163
Carmel, CA 93922

Olivia de Havilland (actress)
BP 156 74764
Paris, Cedex 16, France

Catherine Deneuve (actress)
10 Avenue George V
75008 Paris, France

Robert De Niro (actor)
c/o Jay Julien
9 E. 41st St.
Suite 1000
New York, NY 10017

John Denver (singer)
9744 Wilshire Blvd.
Suite 400
Los Angeles, CA 90212

Bo Derek (actress)
1888 Century Park East
Suite 1400
Los Angeles, CA 90067

Princess Diana (British royalty)
Kensington Palace
London W8, England

Phyllis Diller (comedienne)
Phil Dil Productions Ltd.
1 Dag Hammarskjold Plaza
New York, NY 10017

Joe DiMaggio (ex-baseball player)
2150 Beach St.
San Francisco, CA 94123

Phil Donahue (TV talk show host)
NBC-TV
30 Rockefeller Plaza
New York, NY 10020

Kirk Douglas (actor)
Bryna Co.
141 El Camino
Beverly Hills, CA 90212

Michael Douglas (actor, producer)
4000 Warner Blvd.
Burbank, CA 91505

Mike Douglas (TV talk show host)
151 El Camino
Beverly Hills, CA 90212

Robert Duvall (actor)
P.O. Box 784
Alexandria, VA 22313

Shelley Duvall (actress)
4151 Prospect Ave.
Los Angeles, CA 90028

Bob Dylan (singer, songwriter)
Box 264
Cooper Station, NY 10003

Clint Eastwood (actor)
Box 125
Pebble Beach, CA 93958

Linda Evans (actress)
9000 Sunset Blvd.
Suite 1112
Los Angeles, CA 90069

Morgan Fairchild (actress)
P.O. Box 8170
Universal City, CA 91608

Rev. Jerry Falwell (evangelist)
Moral Majority
P.O. Box 190
Forest, VA 24551

Mia Farrow (actress)
135 Central Park West
New York, NY 10023

Farrah Fawcett (actress)
I.C.M.
8899 Beverly Blvd.
Los Angeles, CA 90048

Sally Field (actress)
1888 Century Park East
Suite 1400
Los Angeles, CA 90067

Carrie Fisher (actress)
10350 Santa Monica Blvd.
Suite 210
Los Angeles, CA 90025

Ella Fitzgerald (singer)
c/o Norman Granz
451 N. Canon Drive
Beverly Hills, CA 90210

Jane Fonda (actress)
8642 Melrose Ave.
Suite 200
Los Angeles, CA 90069

Gerald and Betty Ford
(ex-U.S. president)
P.O. Box 927
Rancho Mirage, CA 92270

Harrison Ford (actor)
222 N. Canon Dr.
Suite 204
Beverly Hills, CA 90210

Milos Forman (director)
c/o The Lantz Office
888 7th Ave.
New York, NY 10019

Redd Foxx (comedian, actor)
933 N. La Brea Ave.
Los Angeles, CA 90038

Aretha Franklin (singer)
c/o Rev. Cecil Franklin
16919 Stansbury
Detroit, MI 48235

Bonnie Franklin (actress)
1888 Century Park East
Suite 1400
Los Angeles, CA 90067

John Kenneth Galbraith
(economist)
30 Francis Ave.
Cambridge, MA 02138

Greta Garbo (actress)
450 E. 52nd St.
New York, NY 10022

Ava Gardner (actress)
34 Ennismore Gardens
London, SW7, England

James Garner (actor)
141 El Camino
Suite 110
Beverly Hills, CA 90212

Richard Gere (actor)
545 Madison Ave.
Suite 800
New York, NY 10022

Andy Gibb (singer)
c/o Martin Hewlett
8335 Sunset Blvd.
Los Angeles, CA 90069

Mel Gibson (actor)
151 El Camino
Beverly Hills, CA 90212

Sir John Gielgud (actor)
South Pavilion
Wotten Underwood
Aylesbury, Buckinghamshire,
England

Allen Ginsberg (poet)
261 Columbus Ave.
San Francisco, CA 94133

Benny Goodman (bandleader)
200 E. 66th St.
New York, NY 10021

Cary Grant (actor)
c/o Faberge
1345 Avenue of the Americas
New York, NY 10019

Linda Gray (actress)
3970 Overland Ave.
Culver City, CA 90230

Merv Griffin (TV talk show
host)
1541 N. Vine St.
Hollywood, CA 90028

Sir Alec Guinness (actor)
Kettle Brook Meadows
Petersfield, Hampshire,
England

Bryant Gumbel (TV show host)
NBC-TV
30 Rockefeller Plaza
New York, NY 10020

Larry Hagman (actor)
3970 Overland Ave.
Culver City, CA 90230

Alex Haley (author)
P.O. Box 3338
Beverly Hills, CA 90212

Hall and Oates (rock stars)
c/o Champion Enterprises
130 W. 57th St.
New York, NY 10019

Veronica Hamel (actress)
9000 Sunset Blvd.
Suite 315
Los Angeles, CA 90069

Mark Hamill (actor)
c/o Lucasfilm
P.O. Box 8669
Universal City, CA 91608

George Harrison (ex-Beatle)
Friar Park Road
Henley-on-Thames, England

Rex Harrison (actor)
La Renadiere Carsinje 1252
Geneva, Switzerland

Deborah Harry (rock singer)
1888 Century Park East
Suite 1400
Los Angeles, CA 90067

David Hartman (TV show host)
ABC-TV
7 W. 66th St.
New York, NY 10023

Paul Harvey (radio commentator)
1035 Park Ave.
River Forest, IL 60305

Goldie Hawn (actress)
8642 Melrose Ave.
Los Angeles, CA 90069

Rita Hayworth (actress)
132 Lasky Dr.
Beverly Hills, CA 90212

Jim Henson (puppeteer)
P.O. Box 2495
New York, NY 10001

Katharine Hepburn (actress)
201 Bloomfield Ave.
West Hartford, CT 06117

Charlton Heston (actor)
9255 Sunset Blvd.
Suite 910
Los Angeles, CA 90069

Dustin Hoffman (actor)
315 E. 65th St.
New York, NY 10021

Bob Hope (comedian)
10346 Moorpark
North Hollywood, CA 91602

Lena Horne (singer)
9255 Sunset Blvd.
Suite 318
Los Angeles, CA 90069

Rock Hudson (actor)
151 El Camino
Beverly Hills, CA 90212

King Hussein (ruler of Jordan)
Box 1055
Amman, Jordan

Timothy Hutton (actor)
c/o I.C.M.
8899 Beverly Blvd.
Los Angeles, CA 90048

Julio Iglesias (singer)
9665 Wilshire Blvd.
Suite 200
Beverly Hills, CA 90212

Jeremy Irons (actor)
c/o The Lantz Office
888 7th Ave.
New York, NY 10019

Michael Jackson (singer)
4641 Hayvenhurst Ave.
Encino, CA 91436

Mick Jagger (singer)
Rolling Stones Records
1841 Broadway
New York, NY 10023

Peter Jennings
(TV newscaster)
ABC News
1330 Avenue of the Americas
New York, NY 10019

Pope John Paul II (religious
leader)
Palazzo Apostolico Vatican
Vatican City, Italy

Diane Keaton (actress)
145 Central Park West
New York, NY 10023

Nastassia Kinski (actress)
I.C.M.
8899 Beverly Blvd.
Los Angeles, CA 90048

Robert Klein (comedian)
c/o Rollins and Joffe Inc.
130 W. 57th St.
New York, NY 10019

Ted Koppel (TV newscaster)
ABC News
7 W. 66th St.
New York, NY 10023

Judith Krantz (author)
c/o Morton Janklow
598 Madison Ave.
New York, NY 10022

Irv Kupcinet (columnist)
Chicago Sun-Times
401 Wabash Ave.
Chicago, IL 60611

Charles Kuralt
(TV newscaster)
CBS News
524 W. 57th St.
New York, NY 10019

Hedy Lamarr (actress)
c/o Paul J. Sherman
410 Park Ave.
New York, NY 10022

Burt Lancaster (actor)
8966 Sunset Blvd.
Los Angeles, CA 90069

Jessica Lange (actress)
I.C.M.
8899 Beverly Rd.
Los Angeles, CA 90048

Jack Lemmon (actor)
Jalem Productions
141 El Camino
Suite 201
Beverly Hills, CA 90212

David Letterman (TV show host)
NBC-TV
30 Rockefeller Plaza
New York, NY 10020

Liberace (entertainer)
4993 Wilbur St.
Las Vegas, NV 89119

Andrew Lloyd Webber (composer)
11 West Eaton Place
London SW1, England

Gina Lollobrigida (actress)
Via Appino Antica 223
Rome, Italy

Sophia Loren (actress)
Chalet Daniel Burgenstock
Lucerne, Switzerland

Robert Ludlum (author)
c/o Henry Morrison
58 W. 10th St.
New York, NY 10011

Loretta Lynn (singer)
P.O. Box 23470
Nashville, TN 37202

Paul McCartney (singer, songwriter)
Waterfall Estate
St. Leonard-on-Sea
Sussex, England

John McEnroe (tennis player)
c/o U.S. Tennis Assn.
51 E. 42nd St.
New York, NY 10017

Shirley MacLaine (actress)
9255 Sunset Blvd.
Suite 910
Los Angeles, CA 90069

Barbara Mandrell (singer)
Box 332
Hendersonville, TN 37075

Barry Manilow (singer, songwriter)
P.O. Box 4095
Beverly Hills, CA 90213

Mickey Mantle (ex-baseball player)
5730 Watson Circle
Dallas, TX 75225

Steve Martin (comedian)
7858 Beverly Blvd.
Los Angeles, CA 90048

Marcello Mastroianni (actor)
Via di Porta
San Sebastiano 15
00179 Rome, Italy

Johnny Mathis (singer)
P.O. Box 59278
Los Angeles, CA 90059

Willie Mays (ex-baseball player)
51 Mount Vernon Ln.
Atherton, CA 94025

Arthur Miller (playwright)
Tophet Rd.
Roxbury, CT 06783

45

CELEBRITY ADDRESSES, continued

Liza Minnelli (singer, actress)
8642 Melrose Ave.
Suite 200
Los Angeles, CA 90069

Dudley Moore (actor)
c/o I.C.M.
8899 Beverly Blvd.
Los Angeles, CA 90048

Mary Tyler Moore (actress, producer)
9000 Sunset Blvd.
Suite 315
Los Angeles, CA 90069

Eddie Murphy (comedian)
c/o I.C.M.
8899 Beverly Blvd.
Los Angeles, CA 90048

Bill Murray (comedian)
1888 Century Park East
Suite 1400
Los Angeles, CA 90067

Jim Nabors (actor, singer)
P.O. Box 707
Honokaa, HI 96727

Ralph Nader (consumer advocate)
P.O. Box 19367
Washington, D.C. 20036

Pola Negri (actress)
7731 Broadway
San Antonio, TX 79209

Paul Newman (actor)
9665 Wilshire Blvd.
Suite 200
Beverly Hills, CA 90212

Wayne Newton (entertainer)
c/o Flying Eagle Inc.
4220 Maryland Pkway.
Bldg. B, Suite 401
Las Vegas, NV 89109

Olivia Newton-John (singer)
3575 Cahuenga Blvd. West
Suite 580
Los Angeles, CA 90068

Jack Nicholson (actor)
Bresler and Associates
190 N. Canon Drive
Beverly Hills, CA 90210

Jack Nicklaus (golfer)
321 Northlake Blvd.
North Palm Beach, FL 33403

Richard M. Nixon
(ex-U.S. president)
26 Federal Plaza
New York, NY 10007

Jacqueline Kennedy Onassis
(editor)
Doubleday and Co.
245 Park Ave.
New York, NY 10017

Al Pacino (actor)
c/o William Morris Agency
1350 Avenue of the Americas
New York, NY 10019

Arnold Palmer (golfer)
Box 52
Youngstown, PA 15696

Jane Pauley (TV show host)
NBC-TV
30 Rockefeller Plaza
New York, NY 10020

George Plimpton (editor, author)
541 E. 72nd St.
New York, NY 10021

Prince (rock singer)
P.O. Box 10118
Minneapolis, MN 55401

Victoria Principal (actress)
3970 Overland Ave.
Culver City, CA 90230

Anthony Quinn (actor)
Vigna San Antonio
Cecchi Di Roma, Italy

Dan Rather (TV newscaster)
CBS News
524 W. 57th St.
New York, NY 10019

Harry Reasoner
(TV newscaster)
CBS News
524 57th St.
New York, NY 10019

Robert Redford (actor, director)
Sundance
Provo, UT 84601

Burt Reynolds (actor)
8730 Sunset Blvd.
Suite 201
Los Angeles, CA 90069

Lionel Richie (singer, songwriter)
1112 N. Sherbourne Dr.
Los Angeles, CA 90069

Geraldo Rivera
(TV newscaster)
ABC News
1330 Avenue of the Americas
New York, NY 10019

Joan Rivers (comedienne)
9255 Sunset Blvd.
Suite 1115
Los Angeles, CA 90069

Ginger Rogers (actress)
18745 Highway 62
Eagle Point, OR 97525

Kenny Rogers (singer)
c/o Ken Kragen and Co.
1112 N. Shebourne Dr.
Los Angeles, CA 90069

Linda Ronstadt (singer)
644 N. Doheny Dr.
Los Angeles, CA 90069

Andy Rooney
(TV commentator)
CBS News
524 W. 57th St.
New York, NY 10019

Diana Ross (singer)
151 El Camino
Beverly Hills, CA 90212

CELEBRITY ADDRESSES, continued

Jane Russell (actress)
Box 590
Sedona, AZ 86336

Phyllis Schlafly (activist,
lawyer)
68 Fairmont
Alton, IL 62002

Tom Selleck (actor)
9056 Santa Monica Blvd.
Suite 201
Los Angeles, CA 90069

Omar Sharif (actor)
147-149 Wadour St.
London, W1V 3TB, England

Brooke Shields (model, actress)
P.O. Box B
Haworth, NJ 07641

Frank Sinatra (singer)
8966 Sunset Blvd.
Los Angeles, CA 90069

Liz Smith (columnist)
New York Daily News
220 E. 42nd St.
New York, NY 10017

Tom Snyder (TV newscaster)
ABC-TV
7 Lincoln Square
New York, NY 10023

Suzanne Somers (actress)
927 N. La Cienega Blvd.
Los Angeles, CA 90069

Steven Spielberg (director)
4000 Warner Blvd.
Bldg. 102
Burbank, CA 91505

Dr. Benjamin Spock (author)
P.O. Box N
Rogers, AZ 72756

Sylvester Stallone (actor,
director)
9665 Wilshire Blvd.
Suite 200
Beverly Hills, CA 90212

Ringo Starr (ex-Beatle)
c/o Bruce Grakal
1427 Seventh St.
Santa Monica, CA 90401

Gloria Steinem (feminist
writer, editor, lecturer)
Ms. Magazine
370 Lexington Ave.
New York, NY 10017

James Stewart (actor)
P.O. Box 90
Beverly Hills, CA 90213

Barbra Streisand (singer,
actress)
9255 Sunset Blvd.
Suite 318
Los Angeles, CA 90069

Elizabeth Taylor (actress)
c/o John Springer Assoc.
667 Madison Ave.
New York, NY 10021

Cheryl Tiegs (model)
c/o Nina Blanchard
1717 N. Highland Ave.
Suite 901
Los Angeles, CA 90028

Daniel J. Travanti (actor)
9220 Sunset Blvd.
Suite 202
Los Angeles, CA 90069

John Travolta (actor)
1888 Century Park East
Suite 1400
Los Angeles, CA 90067

Lana Turner (actress)
P.O. Box 69187
Los Angeles, CA 90069

Tina Turner (singer)
151 El Camino
Beverly Hills, CA 90212

Gore Vidal (author)
Via di Torre Argentina 21
Rome, Italy

Barbara Walters
(TV interviewer)
ABC News
1330 Avenue of the Americas
New York, NY 10019

Andy Warhol (painter)
19 E. 32nd St.
New York, NY 10016

Raquel Welch (actress)
146 Central Park West
New York, NY 10023

Dr. Ruth Westheimer (sex
therapist)
WYNY Radio
30 Rockefeller Plaza
Room 252
New York, NY 10020

William Westmoreland
(U.S. general)
P.O. Box 1059
Charleston, SC 29402

Henny Youngman (comedian)
151 El Camino
Beverly Hills, CA 90212

Richard Zanuck (movie
producer)
P.O. Box 900
Beverly Hills, CA 90213

PRISON PEN PALS

Well-known people like Truman Capote, Norman Mailer, William F. Buckley, Jr., and Jerzy Kosinski have all corresponded with convicted murderers who were in prison. You too can dabble and scribble a few words to murderers and would-be murderers. Here are a few addresses:

Juan Corona (mass murderer)
Vacaville State Prison
Vacaville, CA 95688

Lynette "Squeaky" Fromme
(attempted assassin of Gerald R. Ford)
Federal Reformatory for Women
Alderson, WV 24910

John W. Gacy (mass murderer, sex deviate)
Lock Box 711
Menard, IL 62259

Jean Harris (murderer of Dr. Herman Tarnower of Scarsdale Diet fame)
Bedford Hills Correctional Facility
Bedford Hills, NY 10507

John Hinckley, Jr. (attempted assassin of Ronald Reagan)
St. Elizabeth's Hospital
2700 Martin Luther King, Jr. Ave SE
Washington, D.C. 20032

Charles Manson (mass murderer)
California Medical Facility
Vacaville, CA 95688

Richard Speck
Stateville Correctional Center
C01065, S016
P.O. Box 112
Joliet, IL 60434

Sirhan Sirhan (assassin of Robert F. Kennedy)
Soledad State Prison
Soledad, CA 93960

FAMOUS PEOPLE NOT NORMALLY
KNOWN BY THEIR FIRST NAMES

Henry WARREN BEATTY
Ernest INGMAR BERGMAN
Charles Eugene "PAT" BOONE
Edmund Gerald "JERRY" BROWN, JR.
George RICHARD CHAMBERLAIN
Leroy ELDRIDGE CLEAVER
Pierino "PERRY" COMO
Alfred ALISTAIR COOKE
Ruth Elizabeth "BETTE" DAVIS
Morris MAC DAVIS
Dorothy FAYE DUNAWAY
Mary FARRAH FAWCETT
Arthur SIR JOHN GIELGUD
Herbert John "JACKIE" GLEASON
Hugh MARJOE Ross GORTNER
Emmet Evan "VAN" HEFLIN, JR.
Alice "ALI" McGRAW
Terrence Stephen "STEVE" MCQUEEN
George Robert "BOB" NEWHART
James DAVID NIVEN
Patrick RYAN O'NEAL
Olive MARIE OSMOND
Margaret JANE PAULEY
Eldred GREGORY PECK
Charles ROBERT REDFORD, JR.
Ernestine JANE RUSSELL
Christina BROOKE Camille SHIELDS
Robert SARGENT SHRIVER
Marvin NEIL SIMON
Michael SYLVESTER STALLONE
Mary Louise "MERYL" STREEP
Margaret "MARLO" THOMAS
Mary Jean "LILY" TOMLIN
Eugene "GORE" VIDAL
Myron "MIKE" WALLACE
George ORSON WELLES
Howard Andrew "ANDY" WILLIAMS
Clerow "FLIP" WILSON
Mary DEBRA WINGER

FOUR PLUCKY REAL NAMES

REAL NAME

Sandra Dee	Alexandra Zuck
Diana Dors	Diana Fluck
Nina Foch	Nina Fock
Tina Turner	Annie Mae Bullock

WELL-KNOWN MEN WHO WERE NICKNAMED "BUD" OR "BUDDY" AS A YOUTH

Marlon Brando	Merv Griffin
Lloyd Bridges	Burt Reynolds
John Glenn	Calvin Trillin

ONE-NAME CELEBRITIES

Annabella	Halston
Ann-Margret	Heloise
Cantinflas	Hildegarde
Cher	Houdini
Dagmar	Liberace
Dunninger	Odetta
Fabian	Vera-Ellen
Fernandel	

FAMOUS PLACES AND NAMES

David BALTIMORE (Nobel Prize-winning biologist)
Irving BERLIN (songwriter)
Godfrey CAMBRIDGE (actor)
Judy CHICAGO (artist)
Grover CLEVELAND (U.S. president)
John DENVER (singer)
Robert INDIANA (artist)
John IRELAND (actor)
Marian JORDAN (actress)
Burt LANCASTER (actor)
Jack LONDON (author)
Joe MONTANA (pro football player)
Grover WASHINGTON (musician)
Alan WATTS (guru)
Susannah and Michael YORK (actors)

THEY LOOK LIKE A MILLION

One way to be seen by the public every day is to get your portrait on U.S. currency. Admittedly one usually has to be a U.S. president even to be considered for the honor but one fellow you probably never heard of, Salmon P. Chase, Lincoln's secretary of the treasury, made it onto a bill and a big one at that. But then again, Chase helped establish the national banking system started in 1863.

Since 1969 bills larger than $100 have not been issued, but many remain in circulation. Here are the names that go with the faces on bills of all the U.S. denominations:

AMOUNT	PORTRAIT OF:
$1	George Washington
$2	Thomas Jefferson
$5	Abraham Lincoln
$10	Alexander Hamilton
$20	Andrew Jackson
$50	Ulysses S. Grant
$100	Benjamin Franklin
$500	William McKinley
$1,000	Grover Cleveland
$5,000	James Madison
$10,000	Salmon P. Chase
$100,000*	Woodrow Wilson

*Used only for transactions between the Federal Reserve System and the Treasury Department.

LITERARY SALOONS: ELAINE'S RESTAURANT AND THE WASHINGTON SQUARE BAR & GRILL

The bar at 1703 Second Avenue in New York City was your basic Austro-Hungarian pub until April 1963 when Elaine Kaufman, ex-waitress and Greenwich Village restaurant manager, opened up her own place, aptly named Elaine's. Writers began to frequent the place to let off a little steam, and then other glitterati followed. Elaine's became so popular that Greek shipping magnates, movie stars, and politicians became regulars. Even Woody Allen stops by regularly to seek a few hours of anonymity at a front row table. Elaine's is so full of well-known people that once, when Elaine was asked where the men's room was, she replied "Uh . . . go to Michael

Caine and take a right!" Here are some of the writers who have been seen more than a few times at 1703 Second Avenue, usually to the left of Michael Caine and to the right of Jackie O.:

Michael Arlen	Larry L. King
Roy Blount, Jr.	Arthur Kopit
James Brady	Lewis Lapham
Robert Brown	Peter Maas
Christopher Cerf	Norman Mailer
Betty Comden	Willie Morris
Frank Conroy	Frederic Morton
Nora Ephron	Nicholas Pileggi
Jules Feiffer	George Plimpton
Bruce J. Friedman	Jack Richardson
Barbara Goldsmith	Irwin Shaw
Dan Greenberg	Terry Southern
David Halberstam	Peter Stone
Pete Hamill	Gay Talese
A. E. Hotchner	Kurt Vonnegut
Dan Jenkins	

To attempt to make a reservation, call (212) 534-8103.

If you live on the West Coast and can't get to Elaine's, the San Francisco counterpart is the Washington Square Bar & Grill, 1707 Powell Street, presided over by Samuel L. Deitsch, Jr. For reservations call (415) 982-8123.

Halls of Ivy | 4.

FAMOUS WEST POINT ATTENDEES OR GRADUATES

Frank Borman (astronaut)
Dwight Eisenhower (U.S. President)
Timothy Leary (counter-culture leader)
Edgar Allen Poe (writer)
Anastasio Somoza (Nicaraguan leader)
James Whistler (artist)

FAMOUS ANNAPOLIS ATTENDEES OR GRADUATES

R. Buckminster Fuller (inventor, designer)
Jimmy Carter (U.S. President)
Merian C. Cooper (movie producer)
H. Ross Perot (entrepreneur)
John Phillips (singer—"The Mommas and The Papas")

FAMOUS AIR FORCE ACADEMY ATTENDEES

Harry Chapin (songwriter, singer)
Jody Powell (White House aide)

Actor David Niven attended Sandhurst, Britain's equivalent of West Point.

CELEBRITIES WHO ATTENDED MILITARY PREP SCHOOLS

Busby Berkeley (Mohegan Lake Military Academy)
Marlon Brando (Shattuck Military Academy)
John Dean (Staunton Military Academy)
John Frankenheimer (La Salle Military Academy)
Barry Goldwater (Staunton Military Academy)
Gregory Peck (St. John's Military Academy)
George Steinbrenner (Culver Military Academy)
Ted Turner (Georgia Military Academy)

FAMOUS PEOPLE WHO ATTENDED LE ROSEY

Le Rosey, an exclusive boarding school in Switzerland, is a nice place to get an education if rubbing elbows with international royalty and the jet-set rich is a criterion. Here are some international celebs who attended the school:

Aga Khan
Prince Alexander of Yugoslavia
Winston Churchill (son of Sir Winston)
Duke of Kent
King Farouk of Egypt
Richard Helms
The Shah of Iran (he was captain of the tennis team)
Prince Victor Emmanuel of Savoy

PHI BETA KAPPA: THE KEY TO SUCCESS

Phi Beta Kappa is a national American honorary academic society founded in 1776 at the College of William and Mary. It is an acronym for the Greek words *philosophia biou kubernetes,* which mean "philosophy, the guide of life." Those students who are elected to Phi Beta Kappa usually are in the top 5% or 10% of a given college's junior and senior classes. Only about 15,000 people are elected each year. Here are a few well-known people who were given the key to success—a Phi Beta Kappa key:

Louis Auchincloss—Yale
MacGeorge Bundy—Yale
George Bush—Yale
Angela Davis—Brandeis
Elizabeth Dole—Duke
Elizabeth Drew—Wellesley
Cyndy Garvey—Michigan State
Mark Goodson—U. of California (Berkeley)
Christie Hefner—Brandeis
Joseph Heller—New York University
Erica Jong—Barnard
William Kunstler—Yale
Kate Millett—University of Minnesota
Edmund Muskie—Bates College
Diana Nyad—Lake Forest College
Joyce Carol Oates—Syracuse
Claude Pepper—University of Alabama
Larry Pressler—University of South Dakota
Joan Rivers—Barnard
Phyllis Schlafly—Radcliffe
William Shirer—Coe College
B. F. Skinner—Middlebury
William Styron—Duke
Franchot Tone—Cornell
Daniel J. Travanti—University of Wisconsin

CELEBRITIES WHO WERE EXPELLED FROM (OR FLUNKED OUT OF) SCHOOL

Woody Allen

According to Allen, "I cut classes and never did any work at N.Y.U., and I was kicked out in my first semester. My parents were so upset that I enrolled at City College night school."

Candice Bergen

In her book, *Knock Wood,* Candice Bergen commented about her experience at the University of Pennsylvania, "After flunking two classes I was asked to leave school."

Marlon Brando

Brando was expelled from Shattuck Military Academy in Minnesota for setting off a firecracker at the door of a teacher whom he didn't like.

Genevieve Bujold

The actress was expelled from a convent school at age 15 after she was found reading a copy of the play *Fanny.*

Chevy Chase

Expelled from Haverford College in his freshman year, Chase eventually transferred to Bard College.

Julie Christie

Julie Christie was once expelled from school for telling dirty jokes.

Michael Douglas

The actor-producer flunked out of the University of California.

Richard Dreyfuss

At San Fernando State College, Dreyfuss was suspended for arguing with a professor about the merits of Marlon Brando's performance in *Julius Caesar.*

Buckminster Fuller

Fuller was expelled from Harvard twice—once for "irresponsible conduct" and another time for a "lack of sustained interest in the processes within the university."

Katharine Hepburn
Miss Hepburn was suspended from Bryn Mawr College for smoking a cigarette.

Ted Kennedy
The Massachusetts senator was suspended from Harvard during his freshman year when it was discovered that a friend took a Spanish exam for him.

Fran Lebowitz
The cigarette-smoking writer and ex-cab driver was thrown out of high school in Morristown, New Jersey, for "general incorrigibility."

Diana Nyad
The swimming star was expelled from Emory University for parachuting from a dormitory window.

Jody Powell
Former Jimmy Carter aide Jody Powell was discharged from the U.S. Air Force Academy in his senior year when he was caught cheating on a final exam.

Robert Rauschenberg
The artist, who originally wanted to become a pharmacist, was expelled from the University of Texas for refusing to dissect a frog in anatomy class.

FAMOUS ALUMNI AND ALUMNAE OF THE AMERICAN ACADEMY OF DRAMATIC ARTS: THE "HARVARD" OF ACTING SCHOOLS

When Harvard professor Franklin Haven Sargent's recommendation to create a drama department at Harvard was ignored, Sargent decided to start his own drama school, the Lyceum Theatre School for Acting, the first acting school in the English-speaking world. The school was later renamed the New York School of Acting and then renamed again the American Academy of Dramatic Arts. Its alumni have been nominated for 75 Oscars, 58 Tonys, and 92 Emmys—quite an impressive record. Here are some well-known graduates:

Lauren Bacall	Lynda Day George	Don Murray
Jim Backus	Ruth Gordon	Pat O'Brien
Conrad Bain	David Hartman	Tom Poston
Anne Bancroft	Florence Henderson	William Powell
Diana Barrymore	Judd Hirsch	Robert Redford
Eileen Brennan	Sterling Holloway	Don Rickles
Dale Carnegie	David Huddleston	Thelma Ritter
John Cassavetes	Kate Jackson	Jason Robards, Sr.
Diane Cilento	Allen Jenkins	Jason Robards, Jr.
Hume Cronyn	Jennifer Jones	Edward G. Robinson
Robert Cummings	Garson Kanin	Rosalind Russell
Cecil B. De Mille	Grace Kelly	Gary Sandy
William Devane	Sam Levene	John Savage
Danny De Vito	Ron Liebman	John Saxon
Colleen Dewhurst	Cleavon Little	Joseph Schildkraut
Kirk Douglas	Marion Lorne	Renee Taylor
Vince Edwards	Barton MacLane	Spencer Tracy
Florence Eldridge	Guthrie McClintic	Claire Trevor
James Farrentino	Dina Merrill	Robert Walker
Gail Fisher	Elizabeth Montgomery	Peter Weller
Martin Gabel	Agnes Moorehead	James Whitmore, Jr.

SECOND CITY GRADUATES

Started in Chicago in December 1959 by cofounders Paul Sills and Bernie Sahlins, the Second City improvisational comedy troupe became a training ground for many present-day celebrities. Its forerunners, the Playwrights' Theater Club and The Compass Players, included such notables as Mike Nichols, Elaine May, Edward Asner, Jerry Stiller, Anne Meara, and Paul Sand. Comedian Robert Klein commented about his fourteen-month stint there, "Second City was the most important career link in my life." Echoing similar thoughts, comedian David Steinberg, who spent seven years with Second City, said: "It was the best training I could have had." Here is a partial list of entertainers who spent time there:

Alan Arkin
Dan Aykroyd
Jim Belushi
John Belushi
Shelley Berman
Roger Bowen
Danny Breen
Severn Darden
Brian Doyle-Murray
Andrew Duncan
Mary Gross
Barbara Harris
Tim Kazarinsky

Robert Klein
Shelley Long
Andrea Martin
Bill Murray
Gilda Radner
Joan Rivers
Martin Short
David Steinberg
Betty Thomas
Dave Thomas
Eugene Troobnick
George Wendt
Fred Willard

YALE SCHOOL OF DRAMA GRADUATES

Kate Burton
Jill Eikenberry
Julie Harris
Ken Howard
Elia Kazan

Stacy Keach
Robert Klein
Paul Newman
Carry Nye
Meryl Streep

Daniel J. Travanti
Joan Van Ark
Sigourney Weaver
Henry Winkler

NORTHWESTERN UNIVERSITY ALUMNI AND ALUMNAE

Northwestern University, located in Evanston, Illinois, has produced a significant number of successful graduates. Especially known for its drama school, Northwestern has the following well-known people on its alumni roster:

Warren Beatty
Saul Bellow
Richard Benjamin
Karen Black
Anita Bryant
Nancy Dussault

Charlton Heston
Ann-Margret
Patricia Neal
Jerry Orbach
Paula Prentiss
Tony Randall

Before They Made It Big

YOU CAN'T JUDGE AN ACTOR BY A SCREEN TEST

SCREEN TEST COMMENTS

Fred Astaire	"Bald. Can't act. Can't sing. Can dance a little."—*MGM*
Clark Gable	"He looked like a big ape."—*Jack Warner*
Ava Gardner	"She can't talk. She can't act. She's terrific." —*MGM*
Marilyn Monroe	"Can't act. . . . Voice like a tight squeak. . . . Unable even to take refuge in her own insignificance."—*Columbia Pictures*
Jane Russell	"Unphotogenic"—*Fox Studios*
Robert Taylor	"Too skinny"—*United Artists*

CELEBS IN COMMERCIALS BEFORE THEY BECAME FAMOUS

Many actors and actresses appear in television commercials before they become "household words." Here is a sampling of actors who went commercial *before* they became famous:

	COMMERCIAL(S)
F. Murray Abraham	Fruit of the Loom Underwear
John Belushi	Marine Midland Bank
Robbie Benson	Comet cleanser
James Coburn	Remington shavers
James Coco	Drano®
Pam Dawber	Neet® hair remover, Tupperware
Joyce DeWitt	Secret anti-perspirant

CELEBS IN COMMERCIALS BEFORE THEY BECAME FAMOUS, continued

	COMMERCIAL(S)
Jodie Foster	Crest tooth paste, Coppertone® sun tan lotion
Judd Hirsch	Listerine®
Dustin Hoffman	Volkswagen
Cheryl Ladd	American Airlines
Tom Selleck	Pepsi®
Brooke Shields	Band-Aid®
Lily Tomlin	All® detergent
Daniel J. Travanti	Jeep trucks
Henry Winkler	H & R Block, Chef Boy-ar-dee®, Close-up tooth paste

HUMBLE BEGINNINGS: EARLY TV APPEARANCES OF WELL-KNOWN ACTORS

The big movie stars of today were yesterday's TV character actors. They were glad to get work and most of them accepted union "scale" wages. Most of the following actors and actresses, however, are now available for at least $1,000,000 a movie, plus a percentage of the gross. Here are the shows that helped pay their early rent bills:

	TELEVISION PROGRAMS
Warren Beatty	"Suspicion," "The Many Loves of Dobie Gillis," "Studio One," "Kraft Television Theatre"
Charles Bronson	"Alfred Hitchcock Presents," "Gunsmoke," "Have Gun Will Travel," "Bonanza," "The Fugitive," "Dr. Kildare," "The Untouchables," "Rawhide"
Dyan Cannon	"Bat Masterson," "The Untouchables," "Medical Center," "77 Sunset Strip," "Wanted—Dead or Alive"
Robert Duvall	"The Twilight Zone," "Alfred Hitchcock Presents," "The Virginian," "The Untouchables," "The FBI," "The Mod Squad," "Combat," "Voyage to the Bottom of the Sea"

66

Dustin Hoffman	"Naked City," "The Defenders," "The Doctors and the Nurses"
Walter Matthau	"Alfred Hitchcock Presents," "Naked City," "Route 66," "Dr. Kildare"
Jack Nicholson	"Dr. Kildare," "Tales of Wells Fargo," "Hawaiian Eye," "The Andy Griffith Show"
Robert Redford	"The Twilight Zone," "Alfred Hitchcock Presents," "Perry Mason," "Maverick," "Naked City," "The Virginian," "Route 66," "The Untouchables," "Dr. Kildare," "Cheyenne," "Combat"
Burt Reynolds	"Gunsmoke," "Dan August," "The FBI," "Flipper," "Gentle Ben," "Zane Grey Theater," "Hawk"
Katherine Ross	"Gunsmoke," "Ben Casey," "Run for Your Life," "The Big Valley," "The Virginian," "The Alfred Hitchcock Hour"
Jon Voight	"Naked City," "Gunsmoke," "N.Y.P.D.," "The Defenders"

SOAP OPERA CELEBRITIES

Recently it has become chic for well-known actors to appear in "soap operas" but it hasn't always been that way. Soap operas were either starting points for many actors or they were an alternative to social security for veteran actors. The following soap operas provided a good source of income, in any event, and good training for the following actors and actresses:

"All My Children"—Ruth Warrick, Richard Hatch
"Another World"—Shepperd Strudwick, Hugh Marlowe, Ann Sheridan, Billy Dee Williams, Nancy Marchand, Charles Durning
"As the World Turns"—Gloria De Haven, James Earl Jones, Mark Rydell, Ruth Warrick, Patty McCormick
"Dark Shadows"—Joan Bennett, Kate Jackson, Donna McKechnie
"Days of Our Lives"—Macdonald Carey, Susan Oliver, Robert Clary, John Lupton
"The Doctors"—Louise Lasser, John Cullum, Ruth McDevitt
"The Edge of Night"—Larry Hagman, Lynn Redgrave, Tony Roberts, Barry Newman, Scott McKay, Ruby Dee, Jan Miner, Eva Marie Saint

SOAP OPERA CELEBRITIES, continued

"The Guiding Light"—James Earl Jones, Bernard Hughes, Cicely Tyson, Ruby Dee, Sandy Dennis, Joseph Campanella, Diana Hyland

"One Man's Family"—Eva Marie Saint, Tony Randall

"One Life to Live"—Trish Van Devere, Shepperd Strudwick, Al Freeman, Jr., Farley Granger, Peggy Wood

"Love of Life"—Christopher Reeve, Marsha Mason, Paul Michael Glaser, Tony Lo Bianco, Robert Alda, Nancy Marchand, Jan Miner

"Peyton Place"—Dorothy Malone, Lola Albright, Mia Farrow, Ryan O'Neal, Barbara Parkins, Kent Smith, George Macready, Ruth Warrick, Lana Wood, Diana Hyland, Barbara Rush, Ruby Dee, Lee Grant, Gena Rowlands, Dan Duryea, Heather Angel, Leigh Taylor Young

"Search for Tomorrow"—Trish Van Devere, Jill Clayburgh, Sandy Duncan, Don Knotts, Conrad Bain, Lee Grant, Roy Scheider, Hal Linden, George Maharis, Andrea McArdle, Ross Martin, Margaret Hamilton

"The Secret Storm"—Diane Ladd, Alexander Scourby, Troy Donahue, Don Galloway, Diana Muldaur, Roy Scheider, Laurence Luckinbill, Robert Alda

"Where the Heart Is"—Bibi Osterwald, Zohra Lampert, Laurence Luckinbill

"Young Doctor Malone"—Dick Van Patten, Joan Hackett, Ruth McDevitt, Scott McKay

MOVIE EXTRAS WHO BECAME STARS

Theda Bara	Sophia Loren
Gary Cooper	Marilyn Monroe
Marlene Dietrich	David Niven
Clark Gable	Ramon Novarro
Janet Gaynor	Norma Shearer
John Gilbert	Erich von Stroheim
Paulette Goddard	Constance Talmadge
Stewart Granger	Rudolph Valentino
Jean Harlow	Michael Wilding
Harold Lloyd	Loretta Young

NBC PAGES AND GUIDES WHO
LATER BECAME WELL KNOWN

Take an NBC studio tour or go to the taping of a television show at the NBC studios and you will be escorted by young men and women in "monkey suits," as their uniforms are called. These young people, most of them aspiring performers, are called guides, pages, or guidettes, depending on their gender and function, and they work out of the NBC guest relations department, which columnist Walter Winchell called "the West Point of the Airwaves." Winchell had a point. The monkey-suited youngsters often become successful. Here are some well-known people who were once NBC pages or guides:

Ed Begley, Jr.
Richard Benjamin
Harry Carey, Jr.
Schuyler Chapin
Clay Cole
Don Galloway
David Hartman
Ken Howard
Bob Keeshan
Ted Koppel

Gordon MacRae
Regis Philbin
Gene Rayburn
Terry Robards
Eva Marie Saint
Susan Saint James
Willard Scott
Jerry Weintraub
Dennis Wholey

LAWYERS WHO BECAME FAMOUS
IN OTHER CAREERS

Mel Allen (sports announcer)
Rossano Brazzi (actor)
Hoagy Carmichael (songwriter)
Howard Cosell (sports announcer)
Romain Gary (author)
Erle Stanley Gardner (author)
Julio Iglesias (singer)
Meir Kahane (rabbi, founder of the J.D.L.)
Leo McCarey (movie director)
Ozzie Nelson (actor)
James Pike (clergyman)
Otto Preminger (movie director)
Quentin Reynolds (writer)
Geraldo Rivera (TV reporter)
Murray Schisgal (playwright)
John van Druten (playwright)

Honorable mention: Bing Crosby, George S. Kaufman, Estelle Parsons, and Cole Porter studied law but never received degrees.

DOCTORS WHO BECAME FAMOUS
IN OTHER CAREERS

Michael Crichton (writer, movie director)
Armand Hammer (entrepreneur)
Somerset Maugham (writer)
Michael Myers (actor—*Goodbye Columbus*)
Frank Slaughter (writer)
Jules Stein (entrepreneur)
William Carlos Williams (poet)

DENTISTS WHO BECAME FAMOUS
IN OTHER PROFESSIONS

Edgar Buchanan (movie character actor famous for his "slow boil")
Zane Grey (author of *Riders of the Purple Sage*)
Allan Jones (singer who appeared in *A Night at the Opera*)
Cary Middlecoff (golfer who won U.S. Open in 1949)

"MEN OF THE CLOTH" WHO BECAME BETTER KNOWN IN OTHER CAREERS

Horatio Alger, Jr. (author) — Ordained Unitarian minister

Edmund "Jerry" Brown, Jr. (former Calif. governor) — Jesuit Sacred Heart novitiate for 3½ years

John Danforth (former U.S. Senator) — Ordained Episcopal priest

George Foreman (former professional boxer) — "Born-again" Christian and preacher in Humble, Texas

Little Richard (rock 'n' roll singer) — Bible salesman and preacher

Jackie Mason (comedian) — Rabbinical student

Carl Rogers (psychologist) — Attended Union Theological Seminary

Fred "Mr." Rogers (children's TV show host) — Ordained Presbyterian minister and graduate of Pittsburgh Theological Seminary and Christian Theological Seminary

David Steinberg (comedian) — Rabbinical student at Hebrew Theological Seminary

Ben Vereen — Student at Pentacostal Theological Seminary for six months

Alan Watts (counter-culture guru) — Ordained Episcopal priest

HOLLYWOOD ACTRESSES WHO ONCE LIVED AT NEW YORK'S BARBIZON HOTEL

New York City's Barbizon Hotel, now co-ed, was once *the* temporary refuge of aspiring young, out-of-town, single women who moved to New York to start their careers. A surprising number of these ambitious women later became successful in many fields. The following Barbizon alumnae became famous as Hollywood actresses:

Candice Bergen
Joan Crawford
Grace Kelly
Cloris Leachman

Ali McGraw
Liza Minnelli
Gene Tierney

71

What They Believe 6.

CELEBRITY VEGETARIANS

"Ferocity is still characteristic of bulls and other vegetarians."
—George Bernard Shaw

Marisa Berenson
Candice Bergen
George Bernard Shaw
The Captain and Tennille
David Carradine
Bob Dylan
Dick Gregory
George Harrison
Gladys Knight

Mike Love
Peter Max
Yoko Ono
Smokey Robinson
Gloria Swanson
Twiggy
Bill Walton
Dennis Weaver

FAMOUS QUAKERS

Julian Bond
Jorge Luis Borges
Mary Calderone
Herbert Hoover
David Lean

James Michener
Christopher Morley
Richard M. Nixon
Cheryl Tiegs
Jessamyn West

FAMOUS MORMONS

Jack Anderson
Billy Casper
Jack Dempsey
Gene Fullmer
Harmon Killebrew
J. Willard Marriott

Johnny Miller
Merlin Olsen
Donny Osmond
Marie Osmond
George Romney

CELEBRITIES WHO BELIEVE
IN REINCARNATION

PREVIOUS LIFE (LIVES)

Glenn Ford   Piano teacher in Scotland in the 1800s
                    Roman Christian named Flavius, eaten by
                      a lion
                    Member of King Louis XIV's cavalry
                    17th century British sailor
                    Cowboy
Loretta Lynn   Cherokee princess
                    Maid and mistress of King George III
                    Irish woman
                    Rural American housewife
                    Wife of a bedridden old man
                    Male restaurant employee in the 1920s
Shirley MacLaine   Prostitute
                    Court jester beheaded by Louis XV
Greg Morris   King David
Sylvester Stallone Man beheaded by the Jacobins during the
                      French Revolution
                    Monkey in Guatemala
                    American Indian
                    Wolf boy

CELEBRITY SUPERSTITIONS

Show business types are especially superstitious. Dealing with the critics is intimidating enough for them, so performers look for good luck charms or, even better, things to ward off bad luck. For example, here are a few show biz superstitions:

Never open an umbrella on stage.
Never whistle in a dressing room.
Never use real flowers on stage.
Never have yellow in a set or green in a costume.
Canes are lucky on stage but crutches are unlucky.
Never repeat the last line of play dialogue at rehearsal.
Never quote from *Macbeth* or *Hamlet* in a conversation.
Never put a hat on a bed.
Never place shoes on a table.

Wigs are unlucky.

Squeaky shoes are lucky.

Never send out laundry until opening night is over.

Spit in your dancing shoes before putting them on.

And last, but not least, never say "Good luck" to a performer. Say "Break a leg"

Here are a few more superstitions that some celebs have:

Conductor **Leonard Bernstein** kisses his cufflinks before each performance.

Actor **Richard Burton** always wore something red when he appeared on stage for good luck and to protect loved ones. When his children traveled by airplane, he made them wear as much red as possible.

The late writer **Truman Capote** always emptied ashtrays compulsively because he considered it bad luck to have more than three cigarette butts in an ashtray.

The late movie director **John Ford** always wore the same hat, his "lucky hat," when directing films.

Actress and radio personality **Arlene Francis** always wears a special pendant for public appearances as a good luck charm.

Singer **Crystal Gayle** always carries a buckeye and a copper piece with her.

When performing, **Jerry Lewis** carries photographs of his family in his pockets and doesn't carry anything else.

For good luck, actress **Sophia Loren** always tries to wear something red.

For good luck, actor **Peter O'Toole** always tries to wear green socks.

Opera tenor **Luciano Pavarotti** always looks for a bent nail on stage before he feels fully confident in singing.

Comedy team **Jerry Stiller** and **Anne Meara** always eat Italian food before they make television appearances.

Love, Sex, and Marriage   7.

CELEBRITY SEX QUOTES

Maud Adams (After being fired from a movie shoot because she didn't want to expose her breasts)
"I'm very happy with my boobs but they're not for the screen."

Lucie Arnaz
On "What's My Line," after just arriving in New York on a cold wintry night, Lucie told the audience, "I like to froze my nippies off."

Tallulah Bankhead
When she first met author Norman Mailer, she asked him, "Are you the man who can't spell 'fuck'?"

Brigitte Bardot
"[I am] the most important sex symbol of all time."

Sybil Burton (To singer Eddie Fisher)
"Don't worry, Eddie. It will pass. Richard must always have these flings with leading ladies."

Jimmy Carter
"I've looked on a lot of women with lust. I've committed adultery in my heart many times. . . . That doesn't mean that I condemn someone who not only looks on a woman with lust but who leaves his wife and shacks up with someone out of wedlock. Christ says, don't consider yourself better than someone else because one guy screws a whole bunch of women while the other guy is loyal to his wife."

Cher
"My rule of thumb and it's never failed me, is if a man's a good kisser, he's a great f--ker."

Britt Ekland
"I have always been discriminating in the choice of lovers, but once in bed, I am like a slave. I willingly accommodate any demands that are made on me, sparing whips, chains and diversions."

Deborah Ann Fountain (Miss New York State of 1981)
"I went from a 36 bust to a 34 bust. The suit was too big. I couldn't go on stage and represent New York State like that." (She was disqualified from the contest because she padded the top part of her bathing suit.)

Zsa Zsa Gabor
"It's never easy keeping your husband happy. It's much easier to make someone else's husband happy."

Cary Grant
"The best exercise I know of is making love."

Daryl Hall
"The idea of sex with a man doesn't turn me off, but I don't express it. I satisfied my curiosity about that years ago."

Mick Jagger (Regarding Margaret Trudeau)
"You are suggesting I have some sort of romantic attachment. I have no relationship with her, just a passing acquaintance for two nights."

Norman Mailer
"A little bit of rape is good for a man's soul."

Yves Montand
"I think a man can have two, maybe three love affairs while he is married. But three is the absolute maximum. After that you are cheating."

Jack Nicholson

"When women throw themselves at you all the time, sometimes the only way to treat them is badly."

"Where my head is at now, expanding sexuality is not most satisfied through promiscuity but through continuously communicating with someone specifically."

Roman Polanski (After being arrested for the rape of a 13-year-old girl)

"I am used to grief. This is just a trifle."

Elvis Presley

"Ma'am, ah'm not tryin' to be sexy. Ah didn't have any idea of tryin' to sell sex. It's just my way of expressin' how I feel when I move around. It's all leg movement. Ah don't do nothin' with my body."

THE MOST ELIGIBLE*
CELEBRITY BACHELORS

The following well-known men are among the "most eligible bachelors" in the world, according to the press and other celebrity watchers:

BACHELOR (BIRTH YEAR)

Mikhail Baryshnikov (1948)	Edward Koch (1924)
Warren Beatty (1937)	Greg Louganis (1960)
Barry Bostwick (1946)	Julio Iglesias (1940)
Jerry Brown (1938)	Michael Jackson (1958)
George Burns (1896)	Reggie Jackson (1946)
Johnny Carson (1925)	Mick Jagger (1943)
Richard Chamberlain (1935)	Ted Kennedy (1932)
Oscar de la Renta (1932)	John F. Kennedy, Jr. (1960)
Christopher Dodd (1944)	John McEnroe (1959)
Peter Duchin (1937)	Robert McNamara (1916)
Clint Eastwood (1930)	Lee Majors (1940)
Wayne Gretsky (1961)	Joe Montana (1956)
William Hunt (1950)	Eddie Murphy (1961)

---

*Some readers may question how eligible some of the men (e.g., Edward Koch and Michael Jackson) are. They are eligible until proven otherwise... and besides, Elton John eventually got married!

THE MOST ELIGIBLE CELEBRITY BACHELORS,
continued

William Paley (1901)
Jim Palmer (1945)
Prince Albert of Monaco (1958)
Prince Andrew of Windsor (1960)
Prince Reza Pahlavi (1961)
Harry Reasoner (1923)

Burt Reynolds (1936)
Tom Selleck (1945)
Steven Spielberg (1947)
Darryl Strawberry (1962)
Mark Thatcher (1953)
John Warner (1927)

SEXY AND UN-SEXY FAMOUS MEN

Writer Jane O'Reilly drew up lists of sexy and non-sexy men in an article entitled "What Is Sex Appeal?" in *GQ* magazine. Here are the winners and losers:

Sexy Men

Mario Cuomo ("for keeping the faith.")
Robert DeNiro, Dustin Hoffman, and **Al Pacino** ("who are all the same person. Think: Have they ever been seen together?")
Cary Grant ("for being insouciant, debonair. The sexiest man who ever lived.")
Mean Joe Green ("for being kind to kids.")
Norman Mailer ("for trying.")
Tom McGuane ("for the way he looks, the way he writes, and most of all, his voice.")
Laurence Olivier ("for excellence, and one corner of his mouth.")
Itzhak Perlman, Pavarotti, and **Yo-Yo Ma** ("for taking, and giving joy in their own talent.")
Prince Charles ("for proving that age, style, and class triumph over physiognomy.")
Prince ("for his eyeliner.")
Burt Reynolds and **Sean Connery** ("for dimples. World champs.")
Steven Spielberg ("for being so rich.")
Andrew Young ("for his convictions.")

Un-Sexy Men

George Bush ("because he looks like the first husband we all divorced.")
John DeLorean ("would you buy a new car from this man?")

80

Jerry Falwell ("because of his haircut.")
Boy George ("because of his haircut.")
Gary Hart ("because he screws up on dates.")
Ralph Nader ("because of his suits.")
Prince Andrew ("playboys are passé.")
Qaddafi ("because of his attitude.")
Tom Selleck ("because he thinks he is so cute and if he wants to call me (Jane O'Reilly) up I won't be one bit impressed, so there!")
Sly Stallone ("because of his neck size.")
Mr. T. ("because he is a jerk.")
Donald Trump ("his buildings are boring.")
Claus von Bulow ("would you like this man to marry your daughter?")
Andy Warhol ("because he never wanted to be sexy.")

Source: *GQ*, November 1984, reprinted by permission

UNMARRIED CELEBRITIES

Well-Known People Who Never Tied the Knot

Kay Ballard
Warren Beatty
Truman Capote
Richard Chamberlain
Wilt Chamberlain
Julie Christie
Montgomery Clift
Roy Cohn
Greta Garbo
Sir John Gielgud
Lillian Gish
Halston
Marvin Hamlisch
Edward Everett Horton
Tab Hunter
Lauren Hutton

Derek Jacobi
Madeline Kahn
Paul Lynde
Johnny Mathis
Rod McKuen
Sal Mineo
Jim Nabors
Ralph Nader
Ramon Novarro
Mack Sennett
Gloria Steinem
Lily Tomlin
Gore Vidal
Andy Warhol
Clifton Webb
Dave Winfield

CELEBRATED MEN MARRIED TO MUCH YOUNGER WOMEN

	AGE DIFFERENCE
George and Joy Abbott	46 years
Fred and Robyn Astaire	35 years
Yul and Kathy Brynner	37 years
John Derek and Bo Derek	31 years
Cary and Barbara Grant	48 years
Jerry Lee and Kerrie Lewis	27 years
Meshulam Riklis and Pia Zadora	32 years
Frank and Barbara Sinatra	15 years

WELL-KNOWN WOMEN WHO HAVE YOUNGER HUSBANDS OR SWEETHEARTS

	AGE DIFFERENCE
Ursula Andress and Harry Hamlin	15 years
Mary Tyler Moore and Dr. Robert Levine	15 years
Joan Collins and Peter Holm	14 years
Arlene Dahl and Marc Rosen	22 years
Ruth Gordon and Garson Kanin	16 years
Diane Keaton and Jim Foley	10 years
Olivia Newton-John and Matt Lattanzi	11 years
Princess Caroline and Stefan Casiraghi	4 years

CELEBRITIES WHO MARRIED EACH OTHER TWICE

Love is Lovelier the Second Time Around

Lucille Ball and Desi Arnaz
Richard Burton and Elizabeth Taylor
Stan Laurel (he married four women, a total of eight times!)
William and Carol Saroyan*
George C. Scott and Colleen Dewhurst
Robert Wagner and Natalie Wood

---

*Carol Saroyan is now married to actor Walter Matthau

SIXTEEN ACTORS WHO FELL IN LOVE ON THE SET

Actress Bette Davis once observed, "It is not easy to put a rein on your emotions when the director calls, 'Cut!'" The following actors and actresses performed love scenes so convincingly on camera that they didn't stop kissing after the cameras stopped rolling:

Joan Crawford and Clark Gable
Greta Garbo and John Gilbert
Goldie Hawn and Kurt Russell
Katharine Hepburn and Spencer Tracy
Sean Penn and Elizabeth McGovern
Sam Sheppard and Jessica Lange
Mary Steenburgen and Malcolm McDowell
Elizabeth Taylor and Richard Burton

CELEBRATED MALE HOMOSEXUALS

Horatio Alger
W. H. Auden
Brendan Behan
Truman Capote
Montgomery Clift
Jean Cocteau
Noel Coward
Harvey Fierstein
Jean Genet
André Gide
Allen Ginsberg
Dag Hammarskjöld
Lorenz Hart
Christopher Isherwood
John Maynard Keynes
Charles Laughton
Paul Lynde
Merle Miller
Ramon Novarro
Pier Paolo Pasolini
Cole Porter
Bill Tilden
Clifton Webb
Oscar Wilde
Tennessee Williams

CELEBRATED LESBIANS

Janis Joplin
Kate Millett
Bessie Smith
Gertrude Stein
Alice B. Toklas
Virginia Woolf

CELEBRITY TRANSSEXUALS

Wendy Carlos (formerly Walter Carlos)—Moog synthesizer musician famous for his "Switched-On Bach" recording and score for the movie *A Clockwork Orange.*

Christine Jorgensen (formerly George William Jorgensen, Jr.)—Ex-GI who became a nightclub entertainer.

Jan Morris (formerly James Morris)—British writer and Oxford graduate.

Dr. Renée Richards (formerly Dr. Richard Raskind)—Ophthalmologist who became a professional tennis player on the women's circuit. Her excellent autobiography is entitled *Second Serve.*

Let's Get Physical 8.

THE CELEBRITY PATIENTS OF "DR. FEELGOOD"

Dr. Max Jacobson, a New York physician, became known as "Dr. Feelgood" in the 1950s and 1960s when he treated his patients, often successful people with heavy workloads, with his "vitamin" injections. His patients felt invigorated and word got around that the doctor was a miracle maker. Jacobson became so indispensable that he accompanied Van Cliburn on his second Russian concert and was with President John F. Kennedy at the summit conference in Vienna. Unfortunately, the injections did not contain only vitamins —they also contained amphetamine or "speed," an addictive drug capable of destroying people when used over a long period of time. Here is a partial list of Dr. Jacobson's "vitamin" shot recipients:

Burt Bacharach	Eartha Kitt
Yul Brynner	Hedy Lamarr
Truman Capote	Gertrude Lawrence
Pablo Casals	Margaret Leighton
Maurice Chevalier	Alan Jay Lerner
Van Cliburn	Johnny Mathis
Montgomery Clift	Zero Mostel
Bette Davis	Mike Nichols
Cecil B. De Mille	Jackie Kennedy Onassis
Marlene Dietrich	Senator Claude Pepper
Katherine Dunham	Otto Preminger
Eddie Fisher	Lee Radziwill
Hermione Gingold	Elizabeth Taylor
Sheilah Graham	Andy Williams
John F. Kennedy	Tennessee Williams

P.S. After nearly two-and-a-half years of investigation, Dr. Jacobson's license to practice medicine was revoked by the New York State Board of Regents. He was found guilty of 48 counts of unprofessional conduct in eleven specifications and one count of fraud. Source: *Choice People* by A. E. Hotchner, William Morrow and Co., 1984.

FAMOUS FACE-LIFTS

Jean-Pierre Aumont
Lucille Ball
Rosalyn Carter
Gary Cooper
Joan Crawford
Marlene Dietrich
Phyllis Diller
Kirk Douglas
Henry Fonda
Jackie Gleason
Rita Hayworth
Michael Jackson

Dean Martin
Jackie Onassis
Mary Pickford
Elvis Presley
Debbie Reynolds
Joan Rivers
Frank Sinatra
Liz Smith
Barbara Stanwyck
Elizabeth Taylor
Lana Turner
Barbara Walters

NEW FACES ON THE SILVER SCREEN

**Actors Whose Faces Were Reconstructed
by Plastic Surgery After Accidents**

Montgomery Clift
Mark Hamill
Carole Lombard

Merle Oberon
Jack Palance
Edward G. Robinson

FAMOUS PEOPLE WHO
HAVE NOT HAD NOSE JOBS

Nose jobs (rhinoplasty) in the 1980s are more common than appendectomies were in the 1940s but *some* stalwart, well-beaked famous people have refused to get their nasal cartilage chiseled and rearranged:

Tony Bennett
Jamie Farr
Dustin Hoffman

Karl Malden
Barbra Streisand
Danny Thomas

FAMOUS MEN WHO DON'T WEAR TOUPEES

Not *all* Hollywood leading men and public figures wear toupees to cover up their shortcomings. Here are most of the well-known men who don't wear "rugs" or "scalp doilies":

Yul Brynner
Mr. Clean
Robert Duvall
Mayor Edward Koch

Gavin McLeod
Don Rickles
Telly Savalas

CELEBRITY REDHEADS

Mary Astor
Red Auerbach
Amanda Blake
Teresa Brewer
Red Buttons
James Cagney
Peggy Cass
Van Cliburn
Arlene Dahl
Rhonda Fleming
Jane Fonda
Redd Foxx
Elinor Glyn
Arthur Godfrey
Rita Hayworth
Van Johnson
Abbe Lane
Rod Laver

Vivien Leigh
Myrna Loy
Jeannette MacDonald
Sheila MacRae
Jayne Meadows
Agnes Moorehead
Maureen O'Hara
Jill St. John
Red Schoendienst
George Bernard Shaw
Ann Sheridan
Beverly Sills
Red Skelton
Red Smith
Svetlana Stalin
Gwen Verdon
Alex Webster

BLIND ENTERTAINERS

Ray Charles
José Feliciano
Ronnie Milsap
George Shearing

Edgar Winter (legally)
Johnny Winter (legally)
Stevie Wonder

CELEBRITY SHOE SIZES

You can't judge a man by the size of his shoe but you can judge the size of his shoe if his footprint is permanently on display at Mann's (formerly Grauman's) Chinese Theater in Hollywood. Here are the shoe sizes of a few actors and singers:

	SHOE SIZE
Richard Kiel ("Jaws")	16
Gary Cooper	14
Bob Hope	13
Clark Cable	12½
Cary Grant	12
Dean Martin	11½
Frank Sinatra	11
Fred Astaire	10½
Humphrey Bogart	10½
Al Jolson	9
Jack Benny	9
Edward G. Robinson	8½
Bing Crosby	7½

BAD HABITS, FORMER BAD HABITS, AND SUCH

Warren Beatty	tardiness
Jeff Bridges	talks in his sleep
Mel Brooks	using four-letter words
Ray Charles	ex-drug addict
Errol Flynn	nail biter
Bob Fosse	nail biter
Lauren Hutton	using foul language
Jack Klugman	gambling, ex-five pack a day cigarette smoker
Johnny Mathis	nail biter
Liza Minnelli	nail biter
Paul Newman	heavy beer drinker but works it off
Steven Spielberg	nail biter
James Taylor	ex-heroin addict
Jonathan Winters	ex-heavy drinker

Source: Christopher Andersen's *The People Book*

ADMITTED OR KNOWN ADDICTS

The following famous people have either admitted having or are known to have had a drug dependency at some time:

Eileen Brennan (painkillers)
Ray Charles
Tony Curtis (cocaine)
Blake Edwards (morphine)
The Everly Brothers (amphetamines)
Eddie Fisher (amphetamines)
Betty Hutton ("uppers and downers")

George Kirby
Jerry Lewis (Percodan)
Little Richard (heroin, LSD)
Joe Louis (cocaine)
Bela Lugosi (morphine)
Frankie Lymon (heroin)
James Taylor (heroin)

ON THE WAGON

Humphrey Bogart often said that he never trusted anyone who didn't drink. Many of the following well-known people know better. They've had some problems and they're "on the wagon":

June Allyson
Sid Caesar
Billy Carter
Gary Crosby
Tony Curtis
Shecky Greene
Rita Hayworth
Wilbur Mills
Robert Mitchum
Mary Tyler Moore

Don Newcombe
Jason Robards, Jr.
Doc Severinsen
Grace Slick
Gale Storm
Liz Taylor
Peter Townshend
Daniel J. Travanti
Tom Tryon
Dennis Wholey

Note: For some first-hand stories about celebrities' dealing with their alcohol problems, read television interviewer Dennis Wholey's book *The Courage to Change* (Houghton Mifflin, 1984).

CELEBRITY CHAIN-SMOKERS

The following well-known people are or once were considered to be heavy or "chain" smokers:

Robert Blake
David Bowie
James Coburn
Bette Davis
Michael Douglas
Aretha Franklin
Arlo Guthrie
Audrey Hepburn
Rock Hudson
Bianca Jagger
Mick Jagger
Jack Klugman
Louise Lasser
Jerry Lewis
Dean Martin
Lee Marvin
Marcello Mastroianni
Meat Loaf

Melina Mercouri
Bette Midler
Mary Tyler Moore
Mike Nichols
Jack Nicholson
Harold Robbins
Cliff Robertson
George C. Scott
Omar Sharif
Frank Sinatra
Tom Snyder
Stephen Sondheim
Gloria Steinem
Sally Struthers
Donald Sutherland
James Taylor
Mike Wallace

CELEBRITY PATIENTS
AT THE BETTY FORD CENTER

The Betty Ford Center in Rancho Mirage, California, is rapidly becoming a way station for celebrities making a concerted effort to eliminate a bad habit or two or for other health-related reasons. Here are some well-known people who have plunked down $6,000 for the minimum four-week stay:

Eileen Brennan
Johnny Cash
Tony Curtis
Peter Lawford

Liza Minnelli
Robert Mitchum
Elizabeth Taylor
Mary Tyler Moore

90

HEAVYWEIGHT CELEBRITIES

If each of the following men hasn't weighed around 300 pounds at one time, he has certainly come close to it:

Fatty Arbuckle
Brendan Behan
James Beard
Victor Buono
Raymond Burr
King Farouk
Billy Gilbert
Jackie Gleason
Sydney Greenstreet

Oliver Hardy
Al Hirt
Burl Ives
Herman Kahn
Zero Mostel
Walter Slezak
Fats Waller
Orson Welles
Paul Whiteman

FAMOUS MEN WHO WEIGH
150 POUNDS OR LESS

	WEIGHT (POUNDS)
Alan Arkin	150
Mikhail Baryshnikov	150
Mel Brooks	150
George Carlin	150
Robert DeNiro	150
John Denver	150
Andy Gibb	150
Mark Hamill	150
Mick Jagger	150
Steve Martin	150
Johnny Mathis	150
Bob Newhart	150
Paul Newman	150
Tony Randall	150
Ringo Starr	150
David Bowie	145
Dick Clark	145
George Harrison	145
Elton John	145
Al Pacino	145
Bruce Springsteen	145
Robin Williams	145
Henry Winkler	145
Dick Cavett	140
Michael Jackson	140
Lou Rawls	140
Andy Warhol	140
Paul Williams	140
Menachem Begin	135
Rod Stewart	135
Bob Dylan	130
Woody Allen	120
Sammy Davis, Jr.	115
Leo Sayer	100

TALL WELL-KNOWN MEN WHO ARE NOT PRO BASKETBALL PLAYERS

	HEIGHT		HEIGHT
Richard Kiel	7'2"	Tom Snyder	6'4"
Michael Crichton	6'9"	John Wayne	6'4"
John Kenneth Galbraith	6'8"	Orson Welles	6'3½"
James Arness	6'6"	Muhammad Ali	6'3"
Tommy Tune	6'6"	James Beard	6'3"
Sen. Bill Bradley	6'5"	Gary Cooper	6'3"
Sterling Hayden	6'5"	Jimmy Dean	6'3"
Ken Howard	6'5"	James Dickey	6'3"
Bowie Kuhn	6'5"	James Garner	6'3"
Chevy Chase	6'4"	Elliott Gould	6'3"
Clint Eastwood	6'3"	John V. Lindsay	6'3"
John Gavin	6'4"	Ed McMahon	6'3"
Louis Gossett	6'4"	Roger Moore	6'3"
Harvey Korman	6'4"	Peter O'Toole	6'3"
Ralph Nader	6'4"	Vincent Price	6'3"
Gregory Peck	6'4"	Willard Scott	6'3"
George Plimpton	6'4"	McLean Stevenson	6'3"
Robert Ryan	6'4"	James Stewart	6'3"
Tom Selleck	6'4"	Jon Voight	6'3"

TALL WELL-KNOWN WOMEN

	HEIGHT		HEIGHT
Julia Child	6'2"	Kate Jackson	5'9½"
Lynda Carter	6'	Ali McGraw	5'9½"
Margaux Hemingway	6'	Lauren Bacall	5'9"
Verushka	6'	Shirley MacLaine	5'9"
Susan Anton	5'11½"	Carol Channing	5'8½"
Bea Arthur	5'11"	Cher	5'8½"
Angela Lansbury	5'11"	Jill Clayburgh	5'8½"
Vanessa Redgrave	5'11"	Sophia Loren	5'8½"
Brooke Shields	5'11"	Gloria Steinem	5'8½"
Toni Tenille	5'11"	Anne Bancroft	5'8"
Ingrid Bergman	5'10½"	Rita Coolidge	5'8"
Mariel Hemingway	5'10½"	Donna Fargo	5'8"
Lori Singer	5'10½"	Greta Garbo	5'8"
Lily Tomlin	5'10"	Lauren Hutton	5'8"

FAMOUS NON-TALL MEN

To say that the following men are short, some folks think, is to insult them, therefore, we are calling them non-tall. Some of them are actually shorter than listed but a press agent's job is to make his client seem big in more ways than one.

	HEIGHT		HEIGHT
Billy Joel	5'8"	George Gobel	5'5½"
Norman Mailer	5'8"	Sen. John Tower	5'5½"
Robert Morse	5'8"	Peter Lorre	5'5"
Bob Newhart	5'8"	Alan Ladd	5'4½"
Ringo Starr	5'8"	Roman Polanski	5'4"
Robin Williams	5'8"	Charles Aznavour	5'3"
Lee Trevino	5'7½"	Mickey Rooney	5'3"
Humphrey Bogart	5'7"	Paul Williams	5'2"
Dick Cavett	5'7"	Danny DeVito	5'
Garry Moore	5'7"	Willie Shoemaker	4'11"
Claude Rains	5'7"	Herve Villechaize	3'10"
Edward G. Robinson	5'7"	Gary Coleman	3'7"
Paul Anka	5'6"	Michu	2'9"
Sammy Davis, Jr.	5'6"	Kenny Baker	2'8"
Dustin Hoffman	5'6"		

NON-TALL WELL-KNOWN WOMEN

	HEIGHT		HEIGHT
Sally Field	5'2"	Sheena Easton	5'1"
Eva Gabor	5'2"	Carrie Fisher	5'1"
Sonja Henie	5'2"	Debbie Reynolds	5'1"
Veronica Lake	5'2"	Geraldine Chaplin	5'
Carmen Miranda	5'2"	Patty Duke	5'
Joan Rivers	5'2"	Janet Gaynor	5'
Linda Ronstadt	5'2"	Margaret Hamilton	5'
Sissy Spacek	5'2"	Helen Hayes	5'
Natalie Wood	5'2"	Molly Picon	5'
Connie Francis	5'1½"	Gloria Swanson	4'11"
Petula Clark	5'1"	Charlene Tilton	4'11"
Ruby Dee	5'1"	Nancy Walker	4'11"

CELEBRITY STUTTERERS, STAMMERERS, AND LISPERS*

Stutterers and Stammerers

Juan Belmonte
Marion Davies
John Hammond
Mark Hopkins
James Earl Jones
Henry Luce
Somerset Maugham
Robert Merrill
Marilyn Monroe
Jack Paar
Budd Schulberg
Jimmy Stewart
Mel Tellis

Lispers

Truman Capote
Daffy Duck
Elmer Fudd
Madeline Kahn
Charles Nelson Reilly
Ned Rorem
Sylvester the Cat
Barbara Walters

*Some of these people suffered these impediments only in their youth.

THE U.S. PRESIDENTS BY HEIGHT

PRESIDENT	HEIGHT	PRESIDENT	HEIGHT
Abraham Lincoln	6'4"	Dwight D. Eisenhower	5'10½"
Lyndon B. Johnson	6'3"	Calvin Coolidge	5'10"
Thomas Jefferson	6'2½"	Andrew Johnson	5'10"
Chester A. Arthur	6'2"	Franklin Pierce	5'10"
Franklin D. Roosevelt	6'2"	Theodore Roosevelt	5'10"
George Washington	6'2"	James E. Carter, Jr.	5'9½"
Andrew Jackson	6'1"	Millard Fillmore	5'9"
Ronald Reagan	6'1"	Harry S. Truman	5'9"
James Buchanan	6'	Ulysses S. Grant	5'8½"
Gerald R. Ford	6'	Rutherford B. Hayes	5'8½"
James A. Garfield	6'	William Henry Harrison	5'8"
Warren G. Harding	6'	James K. Polk	5'8"
John F. Kennedy	6'	Zachary Taylor	5'8"
James Monroe	6'	John Adams	5'7"
William Howard Taft	6'	John Quincy Adams	5'7"
John Tyler	6'	William McKinley	5'7"
Richard M. Nixon	5'11½"	Benjamin Harrison	5'6"
Grover Cleveland	5'11"	Martin Van Buren	5'6"
Herbert C. Hoover	5'11"	James Madison	5'4"
Woodrow Wilson	5'11"		

OLDEST TO YOUNGEST U.S. PRESIDENTS
Age at First Inauguration

PRESIDENT	AGE AT INAUGURATION
Ronald W. Reagan	69 years, 349 days
William H. Harrison	68 years, 23 days
James Buchanan	65 years, 315 days
Zachary Taylor	64 years, 100 days
Dwight D. Eisenhower	62 years, 98 days
Andrew Jackson	61 years, 354 days
John Adams	61 years, 125 days
Gerald R. Ford	61 years, 26 days
Harry S Truman	60 years, 309 days
James Monroe	58 years, 310 days
James Madison	57 years, 353 days
Thomas Jefferson	57 years, 325 days
John Q. Adams	57 years, 236 days
George Washington	57 years, 67 days
Andrew Johnson	56 years, 107 days
Woodrow Wilson	56 years, 65 days
Richard M. Nixon	56 years, 11 days
Benjamin Harrison	55 years, 196 days
Warren B. Harding	55 years, 122 days
Lyndon B. Johnson	55 years, 87 days
Herbert Hoover	54 years, 206 days
Rutherford B. Hayes	54 years, 151 days
Martin Van Buren	54 years, 89 days
William McKinley	54 years, 34 days
James E. Carter	52 years, 111 days
Abraham Lincoln	52 years, 20 days
Chester B. Arthur	51 years, 350 days
William H. Taft	51 years, 170 days
Franklin D. Roosevelt	51 years, 33 days
Calvin Coolidge	51 years, 30 days
John Tyler	51 years, 8 days
Millard Fillmore	50 years, 184 days
James Polk	49 years, 122 days
James Garfield	49 years, 105 days
Franklin Pierce	48 years, 101 days
Grover Cleveland	47 years, 351 days
Ulysses S. Grant	46 years, 311 days
John F. Kennedy	43 years, 236 days
Theodore Roosevelt	42 years, 322 days

Wit and Wisdom | 9.

CELEBRITY MIRRORS: SELF-IMAGES

Spiro Agnew
"I think in time the people will come to know what a warm, sweet, lovable person I really am."

Muhammad Ali
"I'm the greatest. I'm the king!
"I am the only man in the world who can go and be loved by the Jews as much as the Moslems."

Lauren Bacall
"It has never been my nature to be competitive."

Tallulah Bankhead
"I'm pure as driven slush."

Rona Barrett
"Underneath, and not far underneath, I'm *too* gentle. I need tenderness and understanding as much as any woman, maybe more."

The Beatles
"We're more popular than Jesus Christ now." (John Lennon)

Yogi Berra
"I never blame myself when I'm not hitting. I just blame the bat and if it keeps up I change bats. After all, if I know it isn't my fault that I'm not hitting, how can I get mad at myself?"

Richard Burton
"You may be as vicious about me as you please. You will only do me justice."

Truman Capote
"I am an alcoholic ... a drug addict ... a homosexual ... a genius."

Billy Carter
"I'm the only sane one in the family."

Dick Cavett
"If I have [an identity] it's a kind of dimpled winsomeness masquerading as sophistication: a combination of wit and earthiness, as if Voltaire and Jane Russell had had a child."

Howard Cosell
"Arrogant, pompous, obnoxious, vain, cruel, persecuting, distasteful, verbose, a show-off. I have been called all of these. Of course, I am."

Walter Cronkite
"I don't know why I'm the most trusted man in America. I'm a very good editor, and CBS News itself is a solid if not stolid entity. But I'll be damned if I know."

John Denver
"I epitomize America."

Federico Fellini
"I'm a liar, but an honest one."

W. C. Fields
"Say anything you like about me except that I drink water."

Barry Goldwater
"I've often said that if I hadn't known Barry Goldwater in 1964 and I had to depend on the press and the cartoons, I'd have voted against the son of a bitch."

Samuel Goldwyn
"I was always an independent even when I had partners."

Katharine Hepburn
"I don't care what is written about me so long as it isn't true."

Edward "Ted" Kennedy
"I was elected president of the Kennedy Foundation because my family thought I should be president of something."

Oscar Levant
"There is a fine line between genius and insanity. I've managed to cross that line."

Norman Mailer
"I've made an ass of myself so many times I often wonder if I am one."

Marilyn Monroe
"I've been on a calendar, but never on time."

Wayne Newton
"Everybody loves me, everybody loves me, but the only one I want to love me is you."

Richard M. Nixon
"Overnominated and underelected."
"I hear that whenever anyone in the White House tells a lie, Nixon gets a royalty."

Sir Laurence Olivier
"I am an actor because that is all I am qualified to do. I shall go on acting until a couple more illnesses cause me to drop. And then I shall write that dreaded book."

Jacqueline Kennedy Onassis
"Anybody who is against me will look like a rat unless I run off with Eddie Fisher."

Sally Rand
"I never made any money till I took off my pants."

Mickey Rooney
"I was a 14-year-old boy for 30 years."

CELEBRITY MIRRORS: SELF-IMAGES, continued

George Segal
"Maybe I play people like lawyers because I'm the only actor in Hollywood who looks as if he could have gotten through law school."

Jacqueline Susann
"A good writer is one who produces books that people read. So if I'm selling millions, I'm good."

Gore Vidal
"Under this cold exterior, once you break through the ice, you find cold water. There is no warm, wonderful person underneath. I am exactly what I seem."

John Wayne
"I'll tell you what I'd like on my tombstone: my name, the years of my birth and death, then three short, simple Spanish words: *feo, fuerte, y formal.* They mean "ugly, strong, and with human dignity.""

Orson Welles
"I started at the top and worked down."

Mae West
"I'm just a campfire girl."

CELEBRITY BLOOPERS

by Johnny Carson
(During a taping of "The Tonight Show," a member of the audience asked Johnny Carson if his wife ever attended the show, to which Carson replied:)
"No, she only comes on anniversaries!"

by Dick Clark
(Introducing a sponsor on "The $10,000 Pyramid")
"Try this delicious *breast* food every morning . . . that should be breakfast food."

by Walter Cronkite

"Prayers were offered throughout the world as Pope Paul planned for prostate surgery at the *Pentagon* . . . that should be the Vatican."

(About the late President Dwight D. Eisenhower) "Apparently the Florida vacation did him a lot of good. Ike returned today looking *fanned* and *tit* . . . that is, tanned and fit."

by Barry Goldwater

(After being asked by Joey Bishop if he'd like to be on his TV show twice a week:) "No, thank you. I'd much rather watch you in bed with my wife."

by Curt Gowdy

"If there's a pile-up there, they'll have to give some of the players artificial *insemination*." (During a football broadcast.)

by Bob Hope

(In response to a woman who just revealed that she was twenty-four years old:) "I've got *balls* older than that . . . of course, I mean *golf* balls!"

by Peter Jennings

"A marine patrol came across the remains of a small VC prison camp near the jungle highlands of *Fuck Doe* . . . that should be Duc Pho."

by Graham Kerr ("The Galloping Gourmet")

"A squid, as you know, of course, has ten testicles . . . ten tentacles!"

about Gladys Knight

(A college campus disc jockey introduced a Gladys Knight record in the following manner:) "And now, rock 'n' roll fans, here's a new record by Gladys Knight and the *Pimps!*"

about Shari Lewis

"One of the bust pepiteers in the business." (Johnny Carson)

CELEBRITY BLOOPERS, continued

by June Lockhart

(On TV's game show "The $10,000 Pyramid," actress June Lockhart had to provide a contestant with some clues for "Things put in the mouth, but not eaten"—and here was June's hint:)

"It's about four to five inches long and you blow it. . . . Oh my God . . . uh . . . it plays music!" (The correct answer was 'harmonica'—or mouth organ.)

about Beverly Sills

"I wish to thank a great talent for appearing on my show . . . Beverly *Hills* . . . I mean opera star Beverly *Sills!*" (Dinah Shore)

MEMORABLE OSCAR SPEECHES AND QUOTATIONS

Julie Andrews

For her award as Best Actress in 1964 *(Mary Poppins)*, Julie announced, "You Americans are famous for your hospitality but this is ridiculous!"

Irving Berlin

Composer Irving Berlin is the only person ever to award himself an Oscar. In accepting the award for his song "White Christmas" at the 1943 ceremony, Berlin said, "I'm glad to present the award. I've known the fellow for years."

Claudette Colbert

Accepting the Best Actress Oscar for *It Happened One Night*, Colbert said, "I'm happy enough to cry but can't take the time to do it. A taxi is waiting outside [for me] with the engine running."

Bing Crosby

For his award as Best Actor in *Going My Way*, Bing Crosby said, "It's the first time anyone ever called me an actor."

Ben Johnson

Johnson, who won Best Supporting Actor for *The Last Picture Show*, humbly said, "It couldn't happen to a nicer fella."

Fredric March

Although Wallace Beery received one less vote than Fredric March for the 1931-32 Oscars, they both won Best Actor awards because at that time a difference of 3 or less votes was considered to be a tie. Acknowledging the coincidence that both March and Beery had adopted children, Fredric March remarked in his acceptance speech, "It seems a little odd that Wally and I were both given awards for the best male performance."

Lee Marvin

In response to his award as Best Actor for *Cat Ballou,* Marvin commented, "Half of this belongs to a horse some place out in the Valley."

David Niven

When a streaker zipped past David Niven at the 1973 awards ceremony, Niven quipped, "Isn't it fascinating to think that probably the only laugh that man will ever get in his life is by stripping off his clothing and showing his shortcomings."

Eva Marie Saint (then pregnant)

After winning the Best Supporting Actress award for her performance in *On the Waterfront,* Eva Marie Saint announced, "I may have the baby right here!"

John Wayne

When 62-year-old John Wayne won his Oscar for the movie *True Grit,* he became the oldest man ever to win the Best Actor award, which prompted him to remark, "If I'd known, I'd have put the eye-patch on 35 years earlier!"

Jane Wyman

Accepting for her Best Actress award as a deaf mute in *Johnny Belinda,* Wyman commented, "I accept this very gratefully for keeping my mouth shut. I think I'll do it again."

BAD REVIEWS

Even the most successful performers get bad notices, and John Simon is by no means the only critic dishing out harsh words. Here are some bad reviews that good actors and singers have gotten through the years:

Jane Alexander
"She's about as Latin as a New England boiled dinner." (Douglas Watt in a 1980 review of the play *Goodbye Fidel*.)

Lauren Bacall
"Phonetically, Miss Bacall is a lot closer to the Grand Concourse than to Piccadilly Circus, and her conception of how a spoiled young English lady might conduct herself is fashioned of the stuff of outright burlesque. . . . It is only by watching her nostrils carefully for an occasional flare that one can get a clue as to how she's feeling at any particular moment." (John McCarten in *The New Yorker* on the movie *Confidential Agent*.)

Tallulah Bankhead
"Tallulah barged down the Nile last night as Cleopatra and sank." (John Mason Brown on Tallulah's performance in *Antony and Cleopatra*.)

"Although Tallulah did not undress, as usual, she lay down on the bed and she got into it, and a maid showed some underclothing. . . . This scene was in the approved Tallulah style—tantrums, and fake tears, and coaxings, and blazing indiscretions. Still, it didn't come off." (Hannen Swaffer in London's *Daily Express* on Bankhead's 1925 performance in *He's Mine*.)

The Beatles
"They are a passing phase. All are symptoms of the uncertainty of the times and the confusion about us." (Rev. Billy Graham.)

Richard Burton
"As for Richard Burton's Caliban, there is no possible explanation, so I will attempt none. He looked like a miner with a tail coming up from a coal face." (A review in London's *Sunday Express* on Burton's 1954 performance in *The Tempest*.)

Julie Christie
"Julie Christie should never, ever, be allowed to sing unaccompanied on stage again." (A Birmingham, England, newspaper review.)

Tom Courtnay

"Tom Courtnay as Charley's Aunt reminded me of Whistler's Mother." (Frank Marcus on Courtnay in a 1971 production of *Charley's Aunt.*)

Jose Ferrer

"Mr. Ferrer likes pauses. He pauses at the slightest provocation. He pauses at the beginning, in the middle, and at the end of every line." (A 1947 review of the play *Cyrano de Bergerac.*)

John Gielgud

"I have always felt that Sir John Gielgud is the finest actor on earth from the neck up." (Kenneth Tynan on Gielgud in a production of *Romeo and Juliet.*)

Farley Granger

"Farley Granger played Mr. Darcy with all the flexibility of a telegraph pole." (Brooks Atkinson on a musical version of *Pride and Prejudice.*)

Helen Hayes

"Fallen archness." (Franklin Pierce Adams on Miss Hayes's 1925 performance in *Caesar and Cleopatra.*)

Katharine Hepburn

"Go to the Martin Beck Theatre and watch Katharine Hepburn run the gamut of emotion from A to B." (Dorothy Parker on Hepburn's 1933 performance in *The Lake.*)

Charlton Heston

". . . a pretty fellow whom the moving pictures should exultantly capture without delay, if they have any respect for the dramatic stage, he duly adjusts his chemise so the audience may swoon over his expansive, hirsute chest and conducts his prize physique about the platform like a physical culture demonstrator." (George Jean Nathan on Heston's 1950 performance in *Design for a Stained Glass Window.*)

James Earl Jones

"Jones sounded like a one-stringed double bass with a faintly Calypso accent, and rolled about like a hugh barrel set in motion by a homunculus within." (John Simon on Jones's performance in a 1965 production of *Coriolanus.*)

BAD REVIEWS, continued

Elvis Presley
"I can tell you flatly, he can't last." (Jackie Gleason)

Maureen Stapleton
"Miss Stapleton played the part as though she had not yet signed the contract with the producer." (George Jean Nathan in a 1953 review of the play *The Emperor's Clothes.*)

Rip Torn
"Torn, playing Eben like a refugee from a Texas lunatic asylum, giggles when he is in despair, stares blankly when he is happy, and spits when he is undecided." (Robert Brustein in a 1963 review of a production of *Desire Under the Elms.*)

THE WORLD (AND OTHER JET-SETTERS) ACCORDING TO TAKI

Taki Theodoracoupoulos, erstwhile "society" columnist for *Esquire* magazine, not only has a way with words but he also has a perspective that most columnists don't have. I mean, let's face it. Hedda Hopper and Louella Parsons, for example, were not children of rich Greeks, they didn't play polo, they didn't have black belts in karate, and they rarely skied in Gstaad. Taki is energetic, cynical, and perceptive—a deadly combination. Here is what he has to say about some well-known people in his columns:

Carter Burden
"The quintessential radical-chic poltroon"

Truman Capote
"The Tiny Terror"

James Earl Carter
"One of the greatest liars and flimflam artists ever to inhabit the White House."

Winston Churchill
"He cared more about port and politics than sex."

Roy Cohn
"The bantamweight but intrepid lawyer, who is as averse to publicity as Margaret Trudeau."

Gossip columnists
"Modern anthropologists"

Anthony Haden-Guest
"The *New York* magazine writer who is well-known among the smart set for his command of the English language and his propensity for passing out before dinner rather than during or after it."

Halston
"The elongated Dracula-like figure whose tastes for the young are well-known ... the transvestite-looking couturier who needs no introduction among gays and rich women."

Juan Carlos of Spain
"The Spanish king's randiness is legendary—but so is his discretion ... Juan Carlos is naughty and is hanging on to his throne by the skin of his teeth."

Nancy Kissinger
"Chainsmoking."

Estée Lauder
"The Queen of Cream"

Swifty Lazar
"A bald-headed midget"

Aristotle Onassis
"The Greek version of Anthony Quinn."

Jackie Kennedy Onassis
"As avaricious as the Aga Khan, as extravagant as the Shah's sisters, and as acquisitive as Elizabeth Taylor during her Burton days."

Roman Polanski
"The pocket Pole paedophile"

THE WORLD (AND OTHER JET-SETTERS)
ACCORDING TO TAKI, continued

Franklin D. Roosevelt
"A secret swinger"

Gunther Sachs
"A hollowed-eyed German with a protruding lip and a cowboy gait."

Taki about Himself
"I was on the Greek Davis Cup Team, won the national doubles about five times, was ranked first in karate until recently, and even skied for Greece. Not bad for a man who prefers nightclubs and booze to fresh air."
"The greatest Greek writer since Aristophanes."

Taki's father
"A great philanderer"

Taki's first wife
"Cristina was a very pretty girl, with a famous name and an unquenchable appetite for low lifers and nightclubs."

Valentino
"The egregious seamstress... Rodolfo Vazelino is what we heterosexuals call him."

Claus von Bulow
"He might have been many things in his life but he was never stupid."

George F. Will
"The only pundit I know who always gets it exactly right."

Tom Wolfe
"The quintessential southern gentleman."

Andrew Young
"Charming, not at all arrogant, but he betrays not a small amount of naivete when he asks me if Melina Mercouri has a chance of becoming the prime minister of Greece."

THE FIRST CARS OF CELEBRITIES

A man never forgets his first car or the first girl with whom he had sex (sometimes in his first car). Here are some celebrities' descriptions of their first cars:

Wilt Chamberlain
"A 1949 black Oldsmobile—the one with the slanted back, not the one with just the humped back. What I did, though, was put on one of those steering-wheel knobs so I could drive with one hand and look really cool."

Lee Iacocca
"A 1938 Ford coupe with 60 horsepower. It was like a large Volkswagen beetle."

Jeremy Irons
"A 1952 side-valve open Morris Minor. Immediately it broke down—in front of the Houses of Parliament. The best thing about that car was that I owned a very reliable bicycle."

G. Gordon Liddy
"A '52 De Soto, and it was a hell of a machine. Cars were cars in those days. The FBI cars, they're nerd-mobiles today."

Paul McCartney
"A dark green classic Ford, bought new with my early Beatles wages.... I used to take my girlfriends out in it. Oh yes, a lot of fun was had in the backseat of that car."

John McEnroe
"An old wreck, a Ford Pinto. My father bought it from one of the partners in his law firm. He paid $100 for it."

Ralph Nader
"I haven't owned a car for over twenty-five years. I've only owned one car—a beat-up white 1949 Studebaker. I'd love to buy another one [car]--if the auto companies met certain standards of safety, efficiency, and pollution control."

THE FIRST CARS OF CELEBRITIES, continued

Dan Rather

"A badly used, and abused, 1939 Ford. We named the car 'the Thing.' The Thing became the talk of the town, partly because the brakes were constantly going and partly because it crashed into several campus buildings."

Ronald Reagan

"A new 1934 Nash. When I got the car, I was working as a sports announcer at WHO radio in Des Moines, Iowa."

Andy Warhol

"I didn't get my first car when I was 16, I got it when I was 56. I got it last year when I was learning to drive. Actually, I got two cars; one's a 1937 Rolls-Royce, the other's a 1970-something Rolls-Royce."

Tom Wolfe

"A 1953 Ford Country Squire station wagon. It constantly grew mushrooms out of the wood. . . . It would get wet and these mushrooms would grow and grow. It was a very strange car."

Source: *GQ*, July 1984, p. 141, copyright © 1984 by Marion Long, reprinted by permission.

QUOTATIONS ABOUT CELEBRITIES

Spiro Agnew
"Nixon's Nixon."—Eugene McCarthy

Fred Astaire
"Astaire is remote. It is as if he were in an incubator, breathing his own air. His perfection is like crystal: you can see through it. It is hopeless to try to imitate him."—Mikhail Baryshnikov

Tallulah Bankhead
"A day away from Tallulah is like a month in the country."—Howard Dietz

Brigitte Bardot

"The only woman I've had a sexual fantasy about is Brigitte Bardot. With me, looks come first, and she's everything a woman should be . . . blonde, beautiful. She's got the most incredible legs—everything. And she's French as well."—Rod Stewart

Warren Beatty

"Warren's conquests of women are not totally successful. His percentage is about fifty-fifty."—Lee Grant

"Warren was the most divine lover of all. His libido was as lethal as high octane gas. I had never known such pleasure and passion in my life. Warren could handle women as smoothly as operating an elevator. He knew exactly where to locate the top button."—Britt Ekland

Leonard Bernstein

"Leonard Bernstein uses music as an accompaniment to his conducting."—Oscar Levant

William F. Buckley, Jr.

"We have three things in common: Irish wives, the ability to speak for 17 minutes without using a verb, and the fact that we both speak with an accent."—Henry Kissinger

Truman Capote

"Jacqueline Susann with an education."—Jack O'Brian

Howard Cosell

"There have always been mixed emotions about Howard Cosell. Some people hate him like poison—and some people just hate him regular."—Buddy Hackett

John DeLorean

"Really, no one's gonna believe it, but John's a simple man with simple tastes."—Christina Ferrare, a model and DeLorean's ex-wife

James Dickey

"The kind of man that after he has four martinis you want to drop a grenade down his throat."—Burt Reynolds

W. C. Fields

"Any man who hates dogs and babies can't be all bad."—Leo Rosten

111

Jane Fonda
"A fake and a bore!"—Truman Capote

Greta Garbo
"What, when drunk, one sees in other women, one sees in Garbo sober."—Kenneth Tynan

Richard Gere
"He's got a pin-up image—which he hates. The only trouble is whenever they ask him to take his trousers off, he does."—Michael Caine

Barry Goldwater
"He wants to repeal the present and veto the future."—Lyndon B. Johnson

Alfred Hitchcock
"A gentleman farmer who raises goose flesh."—Ingrid Bergman

John Huston
"John, if you weren't the son of my beloved friend Walter, and if you weren't a brilliant writer and a magnificent director, you'd be nothing but a common drunk."—Gregory Ratoff

Edward "Ted" Kennedy
"Ted's a considerate person, especially to women."—Joan Kennedy

John F. Kennedy
"The enviably attractive nephew who wings an Irish ballad for the company and then winsomely disappears before the table-clearing and dishwashing begin."—Lyndon B. Johnson

Robert F. Kennedy
"I can't see that it's wrong to give him a little legal experience before he goes out to practice law."—John F. Kennedy, upon naming Robert as U.S. Attorney General

Billie Jean King
"She's a great player for a gal. But no woman can beat a male player who knows what he's doing. I'm not only interested in glory

112

for my sex, but I also want to set women's lib back twenty years, to get women back into the home, where they belong."—Bobby Riggs

Liberace
"This deadly, winking, sniggering, snuggling, scent-impregnated, chromium-plated, luminous, quivering, giggling, fruit-flavored, mincing, ice-covered heap of mother-love . . . the summit of sex—the pinnacle of Masculine, Feminine, and Neuter."—Cassandra, a London critic

Sophia Loren
"What a subject: her nose is too big, her mouth is too big, she has the composites of all the wrong things, but put them all together and pow! All the natural mistakes of beauty fall together to create a magnificent accident."—Rex Reed

Ron Luciano
"He's the only guy I know of who can make a four-syllable word out of 'Strike.'"—Anonymous

Norman Mailer
"He glamorizes criminality, cultivates a prurient imagination, and luxuriates in the freedom of instinctual claims."—James Atlas

Billy Martin
"Extraordinary Achievement Award to Billy Martin, for having reached the age of 50 without being murdered by someone . . . to the amazement of all who know him."—A plaque in Martin's office

Mary Martin
"She's O.K. if you like talent."—Ethel Merman

Walter Matthau
"He could play anything from Rhett Butler to Scarlett O'Hara." —Billy Wilder

Louis B. Mayer
"The reason so many people turned up at his funeral is that they wanted to make sure he was dead."—Samuel Goldwyn

Marilyn Monroe
"Marilyn Monroe could make both ends meet by posing naked for girlie photographs, the most provocative of which was reproduced

in vivid color on the tip of a best-selling condom."—William Manchester

"[She] was all woman. She had curves in places other women don't even have places."—Cybill Shepherd

Jack Nicklaus

"He can land a long iron as softly as a butterfly with sore feet."—Anonymous

Richard M. Nixon

"That man has no future in American politics. Even Eisenhower will refuse to swallow so much half-baked corn."—Walter Lippmann

"Years from now, he'll be judged very closely to the way he's judged in Europe and Asia now—very positively. This guy is an expert diesel mechanic, everything Carter is not. He's not a candidate for sainthood, but remember, we elected a president, not a pastor."—G. Gordon Liddy

Roman Polanski

"As a director, he was ten times more wonderful than as a lover."—Nastassia Kinski

Elvis Presley

"Elvis is so straight it's unbelievable. He doesn't swear or drink or smoke or anything like that. He could be president."—Peter Fonda

Don Rickles

"[His] chosen weapon is the verbal hand grenade. At his best, he breaks through the bad-taste barrier into a world of sheer outrage where no forbidden thought goes unspoken and where everything spoken is anarchically liberating."—Kenneth Tynan

"I like Don Rickles. But that's because I have no taste."—Frank Sinatra

Meryl Streep

"She looks like a chicken!"—Truman Capote

Ed Sullivan

"Ed Sullivan will be around as long as someone else has talent."—Fred Allen

Jocks and Brains 10.

HALL OF FAMERS

Every season has its heroes in a given sport, but it takes more than flashes in the pan to make it into one of the halls of fame—it takes a good, solid career record, although fans of football's Fran Tarkenton and baseball's Phil Rizzuto may dispute the criteria.

To follow are the Hall of Famers in baseball, football, basketball, golf, and bowling.

The Professional Basketball Hall of Fame

PLAYERS

Paul Arizin	Hal Greer
Thomas Barlow	Ace Gruenig
Elgin Baylor	Cliff Hagan
John Beckman	Victor Hanson
Bennie Borgmann	John Havlicek
Bill Bradley	Nat Holman
Joseph Brennan	Chuck Hyatt
Wilt Chamberlain	William Johnson
Charles Cooper	Sam Jones
Bob Cousy	Moose Krause
Bob Davies	Bob Kurland
Forrest DeBernardi	Joe Lapchick
Dave DeBusschere	Jerry Lucas
Dutch Dehnert	Hank Luisetti
Paul Endacott	Ed Macauley
Bud Foster	Branch McCracken
Max Friedman	Jack McCracken
Joe Fulks	Slater Martin
Lauren Gale	George Mikan
Tom Gola	Stretch Murphy

The Professional Basketball Hall of Fame, continued

PLAYERS

Pat Page
Bob Pettit
Andy Phillip
Jim Pollard
Frank Ramsey
Willis Reed
Oscar Robertson
John S. Roosma
Honey Russell
Bill Russell
Adolph Schayes

Ernest Schmidt
John Schommer
Barney Sedran
Bill Sharman
Christian Steinmetz
Cat Thompson
Jack Twyman
Fuzzy Vandivier
Edward Wachter
Jerry West
John Wooden

COACHES

Red Auerbach
Sam Barry
Ernest Blood
Howard Cann
Dr. H. G. Carlson
Ben Carnevale
Everett Case
Everett Dean
Edgar Diddle
Bruce Drake
Clarence Gaines
Jack Gardner
Slats Gill
Edgar Hickey
Howard Hobson
Hank Iba
Alvin Julian

Frank Keaney
George Keogan
Ward Lambert
Harry Litwack
Kenneth Loeffler
Dutch Lonborg
Arad McCutchan
Frank McGuire
John McLendon
Ray Meyer
Dr. W. E. Meanwell
Pete Newell
Adolph Rupp
Leonard Sachs
Everett Shelton
Dean Smith
John Wooden

REFEREES

James Enright
George Hepbron
George Hoyt
Matthew Kennedy
Lloyd Leith

John Nucatola
Ernest Quigley
J. Dallas Shirley
David Tobey
David Walsh

CONTRIBUTORS

Phog Allen
Clair Bee
Walter Brown
John Bunn
Bob Douglas
Al O. Duer
Cliff Fagan
Harry Fisher
Edward Gottlieb
Dr. L. H. Gulick
Lester Harrison
Dr. Ferenc Hepp
Edward Hickox
Tony Hinkle
Ned Irish
R. W. Jones
Walter Kennedy
Emil Liston
Bill Mokray

Ralph Morgan
Frank Morgenweck
Dr. James Naismith
John O'Brien
Harold Olsen
Maurice Podoloff
H. V. Porter
William Reis
Elmer Ripley
Lynn St. John
Abe Saperstein
Arthur Schabinger
Amos Alonzo Stagg
Edward Steitz
Chuck Taylor
Oswald Tower
Arthur Trester
Clifford Wells
Lou Wilke

The Professional Baseball Hall of Fame

Hank Aaron
Grover C. Alexander
Walt Alston
Cap Anson
Luis Aparicio
Luke Appling
Earl Averill
Home Run Baker
Dave Bancroft
Ernie Banks
Edward G. Barrow
Jake Beckley
Cool Papa Bell
Chief Bender
Yogi Berra
Jim Bottomley
Lou Boudreau
Roger Bresnahan
Lou Brock

Dan Brouthers
Mordecai (Three Finger) Brown
Morgan C. Bulkeley
Jesse C. Burkett
Roy Campanella
Max Carey
Alexander Cartwright
Henry Chadwick
Frank Chance
Happy Chandler
Oscar Charleston
John Chesbro
Fred Clarke
John Clarkson
Roberto Clemente
Ty Cobb
Mickey Cochrane
Eddie Collins
James Collins

117

Earle Combs
Charles A. Comiskey
Jocko Conlan
Thomas H. Connolly
Roger Connor
Stan Coveleski
Sam Crawford
Joe Cronin
Candy Cummings
Kiki Cuyler
Dizzy Dean
Ed Delahanty
Bill Dickey
Martin DiHigo
Joe DiMaggio
Don Drysdale
Hugh Duffy
Billy Evans
John Evers
Buck Ewing
Urban Faber
Bob Feller
Rick Ferrell
Elmer H. Flick
Whitey Ford
Andrew Foster
Jimmie Foxx
Ford Frick
Frank Frisch
Pud Galvin
Lou Gehrig
Charles Gehringer
Bob Gibson
Josh Gibson
Warren Giles
Lefty Gomez
Goose Goslin
Hank Greenberg
Clark Griffin
Burleigh Grimes

Lefty Grove
Chick Hafey
Jesse Haines
Bill Hamilton
Will Harridge
Bucky Harris
Gabby Hartnett
Harry Heilmann
Billy Herman
Harry Hooper
Rogers Hornsby
Waite Hoyt
Cal Hubbard
Carl Hubbell
Miller Huggins
Monte Irvin
Travis Jackson
Hugh Jennings
Byron Johnson
William (Rudy) Johnson
Walter Johnson
Addie Joss
Al Kaline
Timothy Keefe
William Keeler
George Kell
Joe Kelley
George Kelly
King Kelly
Harmon Killebrew
Ralph Kiner
Chuck Klein
Bill Klem
Sandy Koufax
Napoleon Lajoie
Kenesaw M. Landis
Bob Lemon
Buck Leonard
Fred Lindstrom
Pop Lloyd

Al Lopez
Ted Lyons
Joe McCarthy
Thomas McCarthy
Joe McGinnity
John McGraw
Connie Mack
Bill McKechnie
Larry MacPhail
Mickey Mantle
Henry Manush
Rabbit Maranville
Juan Marichal
Rube Marquard
Eddie Mathews
Christy Mathewson
Willie Mays
Joe Medwick
Johnny Mize
Stan Musial
Kid Nichols
James O'Rourke
Mel Ott
Satchel Paige
Herb Pennock
Ed Plank
Charlie Radbourne
Pee Wee Reese
Sam Rice
Branch Rickey
Eppa Rixey
Robin Roberts
Brooks Robinson
Frank Robinson
Jackie Robinson
Wilbert Robinson
Edd Roush
Red Ruffing

Amos Rusie
Babe Ruth
Ray Schalk
Joe Sewell
Al Simmons
George Sisler
Enos (Country) Slaughter
Duke Snider
Warren Spahn
Albert Spalding
Tris Speaker
Casey Stengel
Bill Terry
Sam Thompson
Joe Tinker
Pie Traynor
Dazzy Vance
Arky Vaughan
Rube Waddell
Honus Wagner
Roderick Wallace
Ed Walsh
Lloyd Waner
Paul Waner
John Ward
George Weiss
Mickey Welch
Zach Wheat
Ted Williams
Hoyt Wilhelm
Hack Wilson
George Wright
Harry Wright
Early Wynn
Tom Yawkey
Cy Young
Ross Youngs

The Professional Football Hall of Fame

Herb Adderley
Lance Alworth
Doug Atkins
Morris (Red) Badgro
Cliff Battles
Sammy Baugh
Chuck Bednarik
Bert Bell
Bobby Bell
Raymond Berry
Charles Bidwell
George Blanda
Jim Brown
Paul Brown
Roosevelt Brown
Willie Brown
Dick Butkus
Tony Canadeo
Joe Carr
Guy Chamberlin
Jack Christiansen
Dutch Clark
George Connor
Jim Conzelman
Willie Davis
Art Donovan
Paddy Driscoll
Bill Dudley
Turk Edwards
Weeb Ewbank
Tom Fears
Ray Flaherty
Len Ford
Dr. Daniel Fortmann
Frank Gatski
Bill George
Frank Gifford
Sid Gillman
Otto Graham
Red Grange

Forrest Gregg
Lou Groza
Joe Guyon
George Halas
Ed Healey
Mel Hein
Pete Henry
Arnold Herber
Bill Hewitt
Clarke Hinkle
Elroy Hirsch
Cal Hubbard
Sam Huff
Lamar Hunt
Don Hutson
Deacon Jones
Sonny Jurgensen
Walt Kiesling
Frank (Bruiser) Kinard
Curly Lambeau
Dick (Night Train) Lane
Yale Lary
Dante Lavelli
Bobby Layne
Tuffy Leemans
Bob Lilly
Vince Lombardi
Sid Luckman
Link Lyman
Tim Mara
Gino Marchetti
George Marshall
Ollie Matson
George McAfee
Mike McCormack
Hugh McElhenny
John (Blood) McNally
Mike Michalske
Wayne Millner
Bobby Mitchell

Ron Mix
Lenny Moore
Marion Motley
George Musso
Bronko Nagurski
Joe Willie Namath
Greasy Neale
Ernie Nevers
Ray Nitschke
Leo Nomellini
Merlin Olsen
Jim Otto
Steve Owen
Clarence (Ace) Parker
Jim Parker
Joe Perry
Pete Pihos
Hugh (Shorty) Ray
Dan Reeves
Jim Ringo
Andy Robustelli
Art Rooney
Pete Roselle
Gale Sayers

Joe Schmidt
O. J. Simpson
Bart Starr
Roger Staubach
Ernie Stautner
Ken Strong
Joe Stydahar
Charlie Taylor
Jim Taylor
Jim Thorpe
Y. A. Tittle
George Trafton
Charlie Trippi
Emlen Tunnell
Clyde (Bulldog) Turner
Norm Van Brocklin
Steve Van Buren
Johnny Unitas
Paul Warfield
Bob Waterfield
Arnie Weinmeister
Bill Willis
Larry Wilson
Alex Wojciechowicz

The Professional Golfers Association Hall of Fame

Willie Anderson
Tommy Armour
Jim Barnes
Patty Berg
Julius Boros
Mike Brady
Billy Burke
Jack Burke, Jr.
Billy Casper
Harry Cooper
Bobby Cruickshank
Jimmy Demaret
Leo Diegel
Edward Dudley
Olin Dutra

Chick Evans
Johnny Farrell
Doug Ford
Vic Ghezzi
Ralph Guldahl
Walter Hagen
M. R. (Chick) Harbert
Chandler Harper
E. J. Harrison
Ben Hogan
Jock Hutchison, Sr.
Bobby Jones
W. Lawson Little
Gene Littler
Lloyd Mangrum

The Professional Golfers Association Hall of Fame, continued

John McDermott	Denny Shute
Fred McLeod	Alex Smith
Cary Middlecoff	Horton Smith
Byron Nelson	MacDonald Smith
Francis Ouimet	Sam Snead
Arnold Palmer	Jerry Travers
Henry Picard	Walter Travis
Johnny Revolta	Roberto de Vicenzo
Paul Runyan	Craig Wood
Gene Sarazen	Mildred (Babe) Zaharis

The Professional Bowlers Association Hall of Fame

PERFORMANCE

Bill Allen	Don Johnson
Glenn Allison	Johnny Petraglia
Earl Anthony	Dick Ritger
Ray Bluth	Carmen Salvino
Nelson Burton, Jr.	Harry Smith
Don Carter	Dave Soutar
Dave Davis	Jim Stefanich
Mike Durbin	Dick Weber
Buzz Fazio	Billy Welu
Billy Hardwick	Wayne Zahn

MERITORIOUS SERVICE

Eddie Elias
Frank Esposito
E. A. "Bud" Fisher
Lou Frantz
Harry Golden
Steve Nagy
Chuck Pezzano
Joe Richards
Chris Schenkel
Lorraine Stitzlein

WORLD CHESS CHAMPIONS

Before 1866 no official championship playoff was conducted. Nevertheless, the strongest players of the day were regarded as world champions. In order, the chess champs have been:

	Francois Philidor (France)
	Alexandre Deschappelles (France)
	Louis de la Bourdonnais (France)
	Howard Staunton (England)
	Adolph Anderssen (Germany)
	Paul Morphy (United States)
1866-1894	Wilhelm Steinitz (Austria)
1894-1921	Dr. Emanuel Lasker (Germany)
1921-1927	José R. Capablanca (Cuba)
1927-1935	Dr. Alexander A. Alekhine (France)
1935-1937	Dr. Max Euwe (Netherlands)
1937-1946	Dr. Alexander Alekhine (France)
1948-1957	Mikhail Botvinnik (USSR)
1957-1958	Vassily Smyslov (USSR)
1958-1959	Mikhail Botvinnik (USSR)
1960-1961	Mikhail Tal (USSR)
1961-1963	Mikhail Botvinnik (USSR)
1963-1969	Tigran Petrosian (USSR)
1969-1972	Boris Spassky (USSR)
1972-1975	Bobby Fischer (U.S.A.)
1975-	Anatoly Karpov (USSR)

... AND PROBABLY NEVER GUESSED ...

Charles Addams
   The cartoonist married his third wife in a cemetery for dogs (his wife is the founder of the Animal Rescue Fund or ARF). His bride wore black because he likes black.

Edward Albee
   The playwright wanted James Mason and Bette Davis to play the lead roles in the movie version of his play *Who's Afraid of Virginia Woolf?*

Woody Allen
   Two hours a day Allen practices playing the clarinet; he often plays at Michael's Pub in New York City on Monday nights.
   The comedian-turned-director also does not enjoy making movies. He dislikes the early wake-ups, the cold weather, and worrying about expenses.

Cleveland Amory
   The 6'4" author, critic, and curmudgeon shines his own shoes and does not tip captains at restaurants, although he does shake their hands.

Julie Andrews
   The British actress made her Broadway debut *(The Boy Friend)* on her 19th birthday.

Fred Astaire
   Pool shark Minnesota Fats ranks Astaire as one of the top five celebrity pool players. Astaire also avoids ballroom dancing and does not consider himself to be a good ballroom dancer.

Rona Barrett
On TV's "The Tonight Show" the gossip columnist admitted to Johnny Carson that she was 23 years old when she first had sexual intercourse.

Saul Bellow
The well-known writer studied anthropology and sociology at Northwestern University.

Jacqueline Bisset
The British actress's house in Benedict Canyon, Los Angeles, was once owned by Clark Gable and Carole Lombard.

Pat Boone
The singer, a man of religion, wears gold chains bearing both Christian and Jewish religious symbols.

Charles Bronson
In his early years, movie actor Bronson wore his sister's dresses because his family was so poor.

Richard Burton
The late actor never read his "notices." He commented, "If they're good, they're never good enough. If they're bad they upset you."

Sammy Cahn
The prolific songwriter was nominated for an Oscar thirteen times before he won one (for the song "High Hopes").

Truman Capote
The late writer, an avowed homosexual, occasionally slept with rich and famous women. He said that "they were always the aggressors."

Johnny Carson
Carson was offered a role in the movie *Blazing Saddles* but turned it down.

Chubby Checker
The singer, whose real name is Ernest Evans, was renamed by Dick Clark's wife who heard Evans imitating Fats Domino (get it: Fats = Chubby; Domino = Checker?).

Jill Clayburgh
The actress, as a youngster, was once caught for shoplifting at Bloomingdale's department store in New York City.

Alistair Cooke
The host of TV's "Masterpiece Theatre" dislikes driving and hasn't owned a car for decades.

Walter Cronkite
The retired CBS anchorman was a sports announcer early in his career.

Kirk Douglas
According to a custom shoemaker in Los Angeles, actor Kirk Douglas wears lifts in his shoes to look taller than he is.

Aretha Franklin
A disc jockey once introduced Miss Franklin as *Urethra* Franklin.

Joe Franklin
The perennially youthful TV talk show host was Tony Curtis's classmate at Benjamin Franklin High School in the Bronx.

George Gobel
The comedian started off his show business career as a country and western singer.

Marvin Hamlisch
Say the secret word and Hamlisch will show you the duck from Groucho Marx's TV show "You Bet Your Life." Groucho gave it to the composer as a gift.

William Holden
The late actor was Ronald Reagan's best man when he married Nancy Davis, now the First Lady.

Ted Koppel
Born in England, ABC's newscaster Ted Koppel became an American citizen in 1963.

Judith Krantz
In case Miss Krantz's readers are interested, Judith and Bo Derek have the same gynecologist.

William Kunstler
The lawyer worked at Macy's department store in the executive trainee program but left after a year.

John Lennon
Neither John Lennon nor any of the other Beatles knew how to read music.

Paul Mazursky
Like Alfred Hitchcock, director Mazursky tries to make an appearance in all his movies.

Arthur Miller
The playwright may be good with words and drama but he flunked algebra three times in high school. (So did Truman Capote!)

Johnny Miller
Even though Miller golfs righty, he is a left-handed person.

Laraine Newman
The first night Laraine Newman spent in New York City, she was robbed.

Jack Nicklaus
The golfing great is color blind. He can't tell red from *green*!

Joe Namath
Joe Willie (Joseph William) Namath wanted to attend the University of Maryland but his *combined* S.A.T. score (730) fell short of the minimum requirement (750) at Maryland so he decided to go to the University of Alabama. Maryland's loss was the Crimson Tide's gain.

Peter O'Toole
In case any women are interested, actor Peter O'Toole does *not* like women who shave under their arms.

Dolly Parton
The petite but buxom country and western singer sometimes totes a .38 revolver for protection.

Nathan Pritikin
Unlike many diet book authors, the late writer was not a medical doctor.

Tony Randall
The Oklahoma-born actor's real name is Leonard Rosenburg.

Nancy Reagan
As a young actress, Nancy Davis (Reagan) briefly dated Clark Gable.

Ronald Reagan
Astrologists worry about President Reagan because he is an Aquarian. All previous Aquarian presidents (Harrison, Lincoln, McKinley, and Franklin D. Roosevelt) died in office.

Robert Redford
The actor-director has been the sewer commissioner for the Provo Canyon in the Wasatch Mountains, Utah.

Brooke Shields
The model-turned-actress was conceived 5 months before her parents were married.

MOVIE ROLES GIVEN TO OTHER
ACTORS AND ACTRESSES

STAR WHO PLAYED THE ROLE	FILM	STAR ORIGINALLY SLATED FOR ROLE
Lew Ayres	*Okay America*	Walter Winchell
John Barrymore	*Romeo and Juliet*	William Powell (Mercutio)
Ingrid Bergman (they switched roles, Ingrid's request)	*Dr. Jekyll and Mr. Hyde*	Lana Turner
Humphrey Bogart	*Dead End*	George Raft
Humphrey Bogart	*High Sierra*	George Raft
Humphrey Bogart	*Casablanca*	George Raft
Humphrey Bogart	*The Maltese Falcon*	George Raft
Humphrey Bogart	*Sabrina*	Cary Grant
Humphrey Bogart	*The Petrified Forest*	Edward G. Robinson
Charles Boyer	*Break of Hearts*	John Barrymore and Francis Lederer (both turned it down)
Yul Brynner	*Solomon and Sheba*	Tyrone Power (deceased)
George Burns	*The Sunshine Boys*	Jack Benny (deceased)
James Cagney	*Yankee Doodle Dandy*	Fred Astaire
James Cagney	*Tribute to a Bad Man*	Spencer Tracy
Mae Clarke	*Frankenstein*	Bette Davis
Claudette Colbert	*It Happened One Night*	Myrna Loy
Joan Crawford	*Mildred Pierce*	Bette Davis and Ann Sheridan (both turned the role down)
Joan Crawford	*They All Kissed the Bride*	Carole Lombard (killed in airplane crash)
Linda Darnell	*Forever Amber*	Peggy Cummins

130

STAR WHO PLAYED THE ROLE	FILM	STAR ORIGINALLY SLATED FOR ROLE
Bette Davis	*All About Eve*	Claudette Colbert
Stuart Erwin	*Viva Villa!*	Lee Tracy
W. C. Fields	*David Copperfield*	Charles Laughton (Micawber)
Harrison Ford	*Raiders of the Lost Ark*	Tom Selleck
Clark Gable	*It Happened One Night*	Robert Montgomery
John Gilbert	*Queen Christina*	Laurence Olivier
Rex Harrison	*My Fair Lady*	Cary Grant (Prof. Higgins)
Olivia de Havilland	*Hush, Hush, Sweet Charlotte*	Joan Crawford
Katharine Hepburn	*State of the Union*	Claudette Colbert
William Holden	*Sunset Boulevard*	Montgomery Clift
Stanley Holloway	*My Fair Lady*	James Cagney (Alfred Doolittle)
Betty Hutton	*Annie Get Your Gun*	Judy Garland
Boris Karloff	*Frankenstein*	Bela Lugosi
Burt Lancaster	*Judgment at Nuremberg*	Laurence Olivier
Fred MacMurray	*The Apartment*	Paul Douglas (deceased)
Fred MacMurray	*Double Indemnity*	George Raft
Eddie Murphy	*Beverly Hills Cop*	Sylvester Stallone
Jack Nicholson	*Easy Rider*	Rip Torn
Edward G. Robinson	*Little Caesar*	Clark Gable
Ginger Rogers	*The Barclays of Broadway*	Judy Garland
George C. Scott	*Patton*	Rod Steiger
Frank Sinatra	*From Here to Eternity*	Eli Wallach
Gloria Swanson	*Sunset Boulevard*	Norma Shearer
Spencer Tracy	*20,000 Years in Sing Sing*	James Cagney
Lana Turner	*Dr. Jekyll and Mr. Hyde*	Ingrid Bergman
Loretta Young	*The Farmer's Daughter*	Ingrid Bergman

SHOW BIZ FOLKS WHO GET STEPPED ON EVERY DAY OF THE WEEK

The Hollywood Walk of Fame

The Hollywood Walk of Fame is one of few "walk-on" parts that any show biz business person ever aspires to. Having a bronze star embedded in pink terrazo on Hollywood Boulevard or Vine Street is an honor that has been bestowed upon about 1,500 movie, television, radio, and recording personalities.

Of course, Gable, Garbo, Grable, et al. are immortalized, as one would expect, but here are some names of people who you might not think have bronze stars on Hollywood or Vine:

Edwin "Buzz" Aldrin	Mickey Gilley
Neil Armstrong	The Globetrotters
The Beach Boys	Sid Grauman
Leonard Bernstein	Hugh Hefner
E. Power Biggs	Harry Houdini
Bill Burrud	Julius La Rosa
Maria Callas	Jack Lescoulie
Glen Campbell	Rod McKuen
Bennett Cerf	Mickey Mouse
Natalie Cole	Rin-Tin-Tin
Michael Collins	Robert Ripley
Alistair Cooke	Sabu
John Derek	Tommy Sands
Thomas Alva Edison	Bill Stern
Max Factor	Arthur Treacher
Kirsten Flagstad	Mike Wallace
Stan Freberg	Slim Whitman
Betty Furness	Florian Zabach
Eva Gabor	

DRAG KINGS: ACTORS WHO HAVE APPEARED IN DRAG

	MOVIE
Charlie Chaplin	*A Woman* (1915)
Charles Ruggles	*Charley's Aunt* (1930)
Eddie Cantor	*Ali Baba Goes to Town* (1937)

132

Jack Benny	*Charley's Aunt* (1941)
William Powell	*Love Crazy* (1941)
Joe E. Brown	*Shut My Big Mouth* (1942)
Lou Costello	*Lost in a Harem* (1944)
Bob Hope	*The Princess and the Pirate* (1944)
Ray Bolger	*Where's Charlie?* (1948)
Cary Grant	*I Was a Male War Bride* (1949)
Jerry Lewis	*At War with the Army* (1950)
Alistair Sim	*The Bells of St. Trinian's* (1954)
Jack Lemmon, Tony Curtis	Some Like It Hot (1959)
Dudley Moore	*Bedazzled* (1968)
Helmut Berger	*The Damned* (1969)
George Sanders	*The Kremlin Letter* (1969)
Michel Serrault	*La Cage aux Folles* (1979)
	La Cage aux Folles II (1981)
John Lithgow	*The World According to Garp* (1982)
Dustin Hoffman	*Tootsie* (1983)

MOVIE ACTRESSES WHO HAVE APPEARED IN DRAG OR THEREABOUTS

	MOVIE
Julie Andrews	*Victor/Victoria* (1982)
Annabella	*Wings of the Morning* (1937)
Louise Brooks	*Beggars of Life* (1936)
Doris Day	*Calamity Jane* (1953)
Marlene Dietrich	*Seven Sinners* (1940)
Katharine Hepburn	*Sylvia Scarlett* (1935)
Miriam Hopkins	*She Loves Me Not* (1934)
Linda Hunt	*The Year of Living Dangerously* (1983)
Merle Oberon	*A Song to Remember* (1945)
Maureen O'Hara	*At Sword's Point* (1952)
Jean Peters	*Anne of the Indies* (1952)
Barbra Streisand	*Yentl* (1983)
Shirley Temple	*Rebecca of Sunnybrook Farm* (1938)

CELEBRITIES WHO ARE STILL AROUND BUT AVOIDING THE SPOTLIGHT

	YEAR BORN
Leon Ames	1903
Jean Arthur	1908
Mary Astor	1906
Lew Ayres	1908
Irving Berlin	1888
Louise Brooks	1906
James Cagney	1899
Lita Grey Chaplin	1908
Mae Clarke	1910
Myron Cohen	1902
Fifi d'Orsay	1908
Irene Dunne	1904
Greta Garbo	1905
Joel McCrea	1905
Dennis Morgan	1910
Loretta Young	1912

OCCUPATIONS OF EX-CHILD MOVIE STARS

	OCCUPATION
Freddie Bartholomew	Advertising executive
Frankie Darro	Bartender
Bobby Driscoll	Clothing salesman
Deanna Durbin	Wife of French film director (Charles David)
Claude Jarman	Public relations executive; opera company manager
Gloria Jean	Restaurant hostess, receptionist
Baby LeRoy	Lifeguard
Spanky McFarland	Hotdog salesman, appliance sales manager
The Mauch twins	Film editors
Mandy Miller	Nanny
Baby Peggy	Writer
Sabu	Furniture businessman

ACTRESSES WHO BECAME NUNS

"Get thee to a nunnery."—*Hamlet*

MOVIE

Dolores Hart	*Where the Boys Are* (1961)
June Haver	*Look for the Silver Lining* (1949), and others
Baby Jane	1930s Universal movies
Colleen Townsend	*When Willie Comes Marching Home* (1950)

RONALD REAGAN'S LEADING LADIES

Not many women can say that they were in a movie with a president of the United States, but here are some of the actresses who played opposite Ronald Reagan in his major movies:

MOVIE

Jane Wyman	*Brother Rat* (1938)
Margaret Lindsay	*Hell's Kitchen* (1939)
Ann Sheridan	*Angels Wash Their Faces* (1939)
Jane Wyman	*Brother Rat and a Baby* (1940)
Jane Wyman	*An Angel from Texas* (1940)
Jane Wyman	*Tugboat Annie Sails Again* (1940)
Olivia de Havilland	*Santa Fe Trail* (1940)
Laraine Day	*The Bad Man* (1941)
Priscilla Lane	*Million Dollar Baby* (1941)
Ann Sheridan	*Kings Row* (1942)
Ann Sheridan	*Juke Girl* (1942)
Joan Leslie	*This is the Army* (1943)
Alexis Smith	*Stallion Road* (1947)
Shirley Temple	*That Hagen Girl* (1947)
Viveca Lindfors	*Night Unto Night* (1949)
Virginia Mayo	*The Girl from Jones Beach* (1949)
Patricia Neal	*John Loves Mary* (1949)
Patricia Neal	*The Hasty Heart* (1950)
Ruth Hussey	*Louisa* (1950)
Ginger Rogers, Doris Day	*Storm Warning* (1951)

	MOVIE
Diana Lynn	*Bedtime for Bonzo* (1951)
Rhonda Fleming	*The Last Outpost* (1951)
Rhonda Fleming	*Hong Kong* (1951)
Virginia Mayo	*She's Working Her Way Through College* (1952)
Doris Day	*The Winning Team* (1952)
Rhonda Fleming	*Tropic Zone* (1953)
Dorothy Malone	*Law and Order* (1953)
Barbara Stanwyck	*Cattle Queen of Montana* (154)
Rhonda Fleming	*Tennessee's Partner* (1954)
Nancy Davis (Reagan)	*Hellcats of the Navy* (1957)
Angie Dickinson	The Killers (1964)

FAMOUS UNKNOWN CELEBRITIES

People Who Have Starred in American Express Commercials

William E. Miller was an unknown in the early 1960s. He ran as Goldwater's vice-presidential candidate in 1964 and still was an unknown. Miller, however, became famous not by running for the nation's second highest office but by appearing in a TV commercial for American Express credit cards ("Do you know me? I ran for Vice President in 1964 . . ."). Few viewers recognized him immediately but the campaign became so successful that he finally did become a celebrity. Here are the "unknowns" who have appeared in the American Express TV commercials:

Mel Blanc
Charles Conrad (astronaut)
The Duke of Bedford
Sam Ervin (U.S. Senator)
Norman Fell
George Gallup
Gunther Gebel-Williams (animal trainer)
Roy Jacuzzi (tub manufacturer)
Rebecca Ann King (Miss America)
John McIver (actor)
William Miller

Mills Brothers
Francine Neff (U.S. Treasurer)
Pele
Itzhak Perlman
Jackson Scholz (*Chariots of Fire* runner)

"LEGENDS" IN THEIR OWN TIME

Celebrities Who Have Appeared in
Blacklama Mink Coat Advertisements

Some people become famous after they appear in ads but Black-lama mink ads require that the "model" be very well-known—known enough to appear in classic ads with the headline "What becomes a Legend most?" No copy other than the name "Black-lama" appears in the ads. Blacklama minks, by the way, are produced by the The Great Lakes Mink Association and are of high quality. Here are the "Legends" who have donned these plush minks in the ads:

Julie Andrews	Peggy Lee
Lauren Bacall	Sophia Loren
Pearl Bailey	Myrna Loy
Lucille Ball	Shirley MacLaine
Brigitte Bardot	Mary Martin
Carol Burnett	Melina Mercouri
Carol Channing	Ethel Merman
Claudette Colbert	Ann Miller
Bette Davis	Liza Minnelli
Marlene Dietrich	Rudolf Nureyev
Faye Dunaway	Luciano Pavarotti
Margot Fonteyn	Leontyne Price
Paulette Goddard	Diana Ross
Martha Graham	Dinah Shore
Helen Hayes	Beverly Sills
Rita Hayworth	Barbara Stanwyck
Lillian Hellman	Barbra Streisand
Lena Horne	Lana Turner
Ruby Keeler	Liv Ullman
Suzy Knickerbocker	Diana Vreeland
Angela Lansbury	Raquel Welch

RADICAL CELEBRITIES: THE CHICAGO 7

The Chicago 7 helped make the 1968 Democratic National Convention a memorable event, to say the least. They stirred up the crowds and the police enough to get arrested for crossing state lines to incite a riot. They were found guilty, but the verdict was eventually overturned by a U.S. Court of Appeals. Here are the names of those infamous "Yippies," some of whom are now "Yuppies":

Rennie Davis
David Dellinger
John Froines
Tom Hayden

Abbie Hoffman
Jerry Rubin
Lee Weiner

FAMOUS PEOPLE WHOSE NAMES
MAY NOT BE HOUSEHOLD WORDS

The following actors and actresses are well-known faces because they are or were seen almost every night in television commercials.

Jack Eagle	The monk/Xerox (he's Jewish!)
Margaret Hamilton	Cora/Maxwell House® coffee ("Wicked Witch of the West")
Joe Higgins	The Sheriff/Dodge
Jan Miner	Madge/Palmolive® dishwashing liquid
Carlos Montalban	"El Exigente"/Savarin® coffee (he's Ricardo's brother)
Clara Peller	The lady in Wendy's ("Where's the beef?")
Billy Scudder	Charlie Chaplin/IBM
Nancy Walker	Rosie/Bounty paper towels
Jesse White	The repairman/Maytag
Dick Wilson	Mr. Whipple/Charmin bathroom tissue
Jane Withers	Josephine the plumber/Comet®

CELEBRITIES WHO JOINED THE SERVICE AT A YOUNG AGE

Art Buchwald	16 years old (U.S. Marines)
William F. Buckley, Jr.	19 years old (U.S. Army)
George Bush	18 years old (U.S. Navy)
Sean Connery	16 years old (British Navy)
James Garner	16 years old (U.S. Army and Merchant Marine)
Robert F. Kennedy	19 years old (U.S. Navy)
Gore Vidal	18 years old (U.S. Army)

CELEBRITY PILOTS

Well-Known People Who Have Private Pilot Licenses or Were Pilots in the Armed Services

F. Lee Bailey
Johnny Carson
Vince Edwards
Merv Griffin
Danny Kaye
B.B. King
Kris Kristofferson
Ed McMahon

Dean-Paul Martin
Christopher Reeve
Cliff Robertson
James Stewart
John Travolta
Treat Williams
Cale Yarborough

CELEBRITIES WHO HELPED KEEP JOHN LENNON IN THE UNITED STATES

Many people forget that Beatle singer and songwriter John Lennon had trouble establishing permanent residency in the United States in the early 1970s because of his radical views and habits. The following are some well-known people who signed Lennon's petition to the U.S. Immigration and Naturalization Service to keep him from being deported:

Fred Astaire
Saul Bellow
Leonard Bernstein
Bob Dylan

Allen Ginsberg
Jack Lemmon
Henry Miller
Kurt Vonnegut, Jr.

FORTY-THREE FAMOUS PEOPLE WHO SANG "WE ARE THE WORLD" TO RAISE MONEY FOR ETHIOPIA

After news of the famine in Ethiopia spread around the world, many groups of people mobilized to raise funds to buy food for the stricken country. One of the groups was the United Support of Artists for Africa. Composed of well-known recording artists and technicians, the group recorded an inspiring song entitled "We Are the World," written by Michael Jackson and Lionel Richie, and produced by Oscar-winning composer Quincy Jones. The proceeds from sales of the record are purchasing shipments of food to be sent to Ethiopia. The cause attracted a star-studded chorus of sympathizers, including the following performers:

Dan Aykroyd
Harry Belafonte
Lindsay Buckingham
Kim Carnes
Ray Charles
Mario Cipollina, The News
Johnny Colla, The News
Bob Dylan
Sheila E.
Bob Geldorf
Bill Gibson, The News
Daryl Hall
Chris Hayes, The News
Sean Hopper, The News
James Ingram
Jackie Jackson
LaToya Jackson
Marlon Jackson
Michael Jackson
Randy Jackson
Tito Jackson
Al Jarreau

Billy Joel
Quincy Jones
Cyndi Lauper
Huey Lewis
Kenny Loggins
Bette Midler
Willie Nelson
John Oates
Jeffrey Osborne
Steve Perry
Anita Pointer
Ruth Pointer
Lionel Richie
Smokey Robinson
Kenny Rogers
Diana Ross
Paul Simon
Bruce Springsteen
Tina Turner
Dionne Warwick
Stevie Wonder

Distinctions 12.

THE TEN MOST BEAUTIFUL WOMEN ON TELEVISION

TV Guide polled a panel of experts to determine the ten most beautiful women who regularly appear on television. The experts included make-up artist Way Bandy, model agents Nina Blanchard and Eileen Ford, portrait photographer George Hurrell, *Vogue* beauty and fitness editor Shirley Lord, and a few other well-qualified beauty mavens. Here are the winners:

Diahann Carroll ("Dynasty")—"Elegant . . . the bones are there . . . more style"

Joan Collins ("Dynasty")—"Bright, energetic . . . **gorgeous** . . . she's done more for women over 40 than the Duchess of Windsor"

Linda Evans ("Dynasty")—"Style, elegance, and a total beauty"

Veronica Hamel ("Hill Street Blues")—"Not only beautiful but shiningly intelligent"

Shari Belafonte-Harper ("Hotel")—"Fine cheekbones and a fabulous smile"

Stefanie Powers ("Hart to Hart")—"Good features . . . enormous vitality . . . wonderful open-air quality . . . a *vital* beauty"

Priscilla Presley ("Dallas")—"Gorgeous, with close to perfect features, a lovely smile and beautiful blue eyes"

Connie Sellecca ("Hotel")—"An interesting dark beauty . . . devastating eyes"

Jane Seymour ("East of Eden")—"Elegance . . . wonderful bearing"

Jaclyn Smith ("Charlie Angels")—"Absolute perfection of bone structure . . . classic features"

Source: *TV Guide*, December 15, 1984

THE TEN MOST BEAUTIFUL WOMEN
ON TELEVISION, continued

Honorable mention: Maud Adams, Valerie Bertinelli, Morgan Brittany, Claudia Cardinale, Lois Chiles, Connie Chung, Morgan Fairchild, Farrah Fawcett, Sharon Gless, Linda Gray, Shelley Hack, Deirdre Hall, Kate Jackson, Heather Locklear, Donna Mills, Jane Pauley, Victoria Principal, Diane Sawyer, Cynthia Sikes, Barbara Walters, Mary Alice Williams, Jane Wyman, and Stephanie Zimbalist.

THE TOP TEN STYLE-MAKERS OF 1984

The 5,200 members of the National Hairdressers and Cosmetologists Association came up with this list of style-makers:

Diahann Carroll	Susan Lucci
Joan Collins	Donna Mills
Sheena Easton	Nancy Reagan
Geraldine Ferraro	Diana Ross
Linda Gray	Elizabeth Taylor

AMERICA'S TWENTY-FIVE MOST
INFLUENTIAL WOMEN

The *World Almanac* polls editors at daily newspapers throughout the United States to determine the most influential women in the country. Of the winners, Geraldine Ferraro, the Democratic nominee for vice-president, received the greatest number of votes:

Arts
Beverly Sills, general director of the New York City Opera
Cathy Guisewite, cartoonist, "Cathy"

Business
Katharine Graham, Washington Post Company board chairman
Mary Kay Ash, founder of Mary Kay Cosmetics

Education, Scholarship, Science
Sally Ride, America's first female astronaut
Barbara Jordan, professor and former congresswoman
Barbara Tuchman, author and historian

142

Entertainment
Jane Fonda, actress and exercise book author
Shirley MacLaine, Oscar-winning actress and author
Katharine Hepburn, four-time Oscar-winning actress

Government
Geraldine Ferraro, Democratic nominee for U.S. vice-president
Sandra Day O'Connor, U.S. Supreme Court justice
Elizabeth Dole, U.S. Secretary of Health and Human Services
Dianne Feinstein, mayor of San Francisco
Nancy Reagan, U.S. "First Lady"
Jeane Kirkpatrick, former U.S. representative to the U.N.

Media
Ellen Goodman, syndicated *Boston Globe* columnist
Ann Landers, syndicated columnist
Erma Bombeck, humorist and syndicated columnist

Social Activists
Gloria Steinem, editor of *Ms.* magazine
Betty Ford, advocate of drug/alcohol abuse treatment and former
    "First Lady"
Phyllis Schlafly, conservative spokeswoman and anti-ERA activist

Sports
Martina Navratilova, five-time Wimbledon tennis champion
Mary Decker, long-distance runner
Chris Evert Lloyd, six-time U.S. women's singles tennis champion

THE MOST ADMIRED WOMEN

Good Housekeeping magazine recently conducted a poll to find
out whom their readers admired the most. Here are the winners:

Princess Diana	Pat Nixon
Elizabeth Dole	Justice Sandra Day O'Connor
Geraldine Ferraro	Nancy Reagan
Jeane Kirkpatrick	Phyllis Schlafly
Mother Teresa	Margaret Thatcher

THE TEN BEST COIFFURED WOMEN OF 1984

(as judged by the Helene Curtis Guild of Professional Hairstylists)

Deborah Adair
Shari Belafonte-Harper
Valerie Bertinelli
Princess Diana
Joan Lunden

Barbara Mandrell
Anne Murray
Joan Rivers
Susan St. James
Connie Sellecca

THE WORST DRESSED WOMEN OF 1984

(according to Mr. Blackwell, the Hollywood designer)

Pamela Blackwood ("Dynasty")—"the living end of the endangered species"

Diahann Carroll and **Joan Collins**—a tie, they take the "Tacky Taste Crown of the 1980s"

Cher—"a plucked cockatoo who has set femininity back 20 years"

Patti Davis (President Reagan's daughter)—"packs all the glamour of an old wornout sneaker"

Sally Field—"'Flying Nun' takes a fashion dive"

Cyndi Lauper—"looks like the aftermath of the San Francisco earthquake"

Prince and **Twisted Sister**—a tie, Prince is "a toothpick wrapped in a purple doily" and Twisted Sister band members are "a Mardi Gras nightmare"

Barbra Streisand—"the Al Capone look with electrocuted hair"

Sharlene Wells (Miss America)—"an armadillo with corn pads"

THE WORST UNDRESSED WOMAN OF 1984

(according to Mr. Blackwell, the Hollywood designer)
former Miss America Vanessa Williams

144

THE BEST- AND WORST-DRESSED

(according to designer Jacques Bellini)

BEST-DRESSED WOMEN

Christie Brinkley
Joan Collins
Princess Diana
Jennifer O'Neill
Nancy Reagan
Joan Rivers
Elizabeth Taylor

WORST-DRESSED WOMEN

Cher
Linda Evans
Geraldine Ferraro
Priscilla Presley
Diana Ross

BEST-DRESSED MEN

Bill Cosby
Cary Grant
Paul McCartney
Prince Charles
Ronald Reagan
Frank Sinatra

WORST-DRESSED MEN

Jesse Jackson
Willie Nelson
Burt Reynolds
Kenny Rogers
Tom Selleck

THE TEN WORST CELEBRITY SHAPES

Personal fitness expert Bill Calkins of *One to One Fitness* in Los Angeles (and trainer for notables like Adrienne Barbeau and James McNichol of "General Hospital") named ten celebrities to his "Worst Shapes Hall of Fame." According to Calkins, "Each of these people set a terrible example and discourage others from looking their best." Of course, Shelley Winters was an obvious nominee. She has appeared on late night talk shows for years, always mentioning that she was overweight because being fat was a requirement for her next film role. Fat chance! Here are some inductees into the "Worst Shapes" Hall of Fame:

Boy George—"Aerobics are murder in high heels"
Merv Griffin—"Celebrity boot-licking doesn't burn calories, and it shows."
Jayne Kennedy—"No butts about it, she should stick to waist up camera shots."
Tip O'Neill—"Eater of the House"

THE TEN WORSE CELEBRITY SHAPES, continued

Ozzy Osbourne—"Definitely not iron man; the only man to find a rat in his fried chicken and eat it anyway."
Dolly Parton—"Udderly too much"
Prince—"Purple wimp"
Joan Rivers—"No competition for Heidi Abramowitz"
Richard Simmons—"What Liberace could have been."
Shelley Winters—"The real reason the *Poseidon* sank."

Honorable Mention

Woody Allen—"When he gets the urge to lie down, he should exercise."
Tommy Lasorda—"It's been said that Tommy Lasagna never met a meal he didn't like."
Charlene Tilton—"She couldn't have shot J.R.; she was at Burger King."
Mr. T.—"Cross between Arnold Schwarzenegger and Fat Albert"

THE TEN MOST HUGGABLE WOMEN

At least these ladies are on the *National Enquirer's* list.* That periodical doesn't say it's somewhat tongue-in-cheek; perhaps these women are most in need of hugs.

Princess Diana	Jacqueline Kennedy Onassis
Queen Elizabeth	Nancy Reagan
Betty Ford	Mother Teresa
Indira Gandhi	Margaret Thatcher
Sandra Day O'Connor	Barbara Walters

*March 6, 1984

THE WORLD'S TEN MOST HUGGABLE PEOPLE

Alan Alda	Ruth Gordon
George Burns	Coretta King
Leo Buscaglia	Pope Paul II
E. T.	Jimmy Stewart
Betty Ford	Lech Walesa

Source: the International Hug Center

THE MOST STYLISH AND LEAST STYLISH MEN

The key to real style, according to W. Rushton Chatsworth III in *GQ* magazine (Jan. '85), is "maintaining your individuality in all your various lives, without imposing your personal tastes, exquisitely evolved as they may be—on others. One must be distinctive without being boorish about it. Here are those well-known men who have real style and those who don't have it, according to *GQ*:

STYLISH
David Bowie
Anthony Burgess
Michael Caine
Placido Domingo
Robert Duvall
Clint Eastwood
Albert Finney
Ken Follett
John Gielgud
Benny Goodman
Cary Grant
Alec Guinness
George Roy Hill
David Hockney
King Juan Carlos
Yves Montand
Jack Nicholson
Gregory Peck
Robert Redford
John Sayles
Sam Shepard

STYLELESSNESS
Mikhail Baryshnikov
Alexander Cohen
Francis Ford Coppola
Mario Cuomo
Alfonse D'Amato
John Kenneth Galbraith
Alexander Godunov
Jesse Helms
Dustin Hoffman
Jeremy Irons
Michael Korda
Rudolf Nureyev
Joseph Papp
Steve Ross
John Warner
"Most top Hollywood studio execs"

THE TEN MOST WATCHABLE
MEN IN THE WORLD

Kirk and Michael Douglas
Mel Gibson
Dave Hasselhof
Jesse Jackson
Ed McMahon

Dean Martin
Joe Montana
President Ronald Reagan
Chuck Woolery

Source: Suzy Mallory, Man Watchers Inc., *USA Today*, December 27, 1984

"FIFTY WHO MADE THE DIFFERENCE"

When *Esquire* magazine recently celebrated its 50th anniversary it decided to devote the Golden Anniversary issue to "Fifty Who Made the Difference"—fifty Americans who "had made a significant difference in today's world through individual effort in their chosen field." These individuals were celebrated "not because they were perfect models of human potential or even because their actions were admirable in all respects, but because in the final analysis they have made a positive difference. Here are the fifty honored Americans:

"TRAILBLAZERS: EXTENDING OUR HORIZONS"

Neil Armstrong
Oswald Avery
George Gallup
Jack Kerouac
Alfred Kinsey
Richard Nixon
Jackie Robinson
John Rock
Jonas Salk

"THE REAL AND THE MYSTIC"

Walt Disney
Lyndon Johnson
John F. Kennedy
Muhammad Ali
Jacqueline Onassis
Elvis Presley

"ARCHITECTS OF THE ENDURING"

Dean Acheson
Dorothy Day
Philip Johnson
John L. Lewis
Henry Luce
J. Robert Oppenheimer
William Paley
the Rockefeller brothers
Thomas Watson

"THE STRENGTH TO PERSEVERE"

Rachel Carson
Betty Friedan
John Khanlian
Malcolm X
Edward R. Murrow
Ralph Nader
Benjamin Spock
Earl Warren
Edmund Wilson
Woodward and Bernstein

"TAKING THE LONG, SHARP VIEW"

Alfred Barr
John Ford
Martin Luther King, Jr.

"SETTING THE STANDARDS"

Dwight D. Eisenhower
Duke Ellington
William Faulkner

F. Scott Fitzgerald
William Levitt
Abraham Maslow
Reinhold Niebuhr
Robert Noyce
Tennessee Williams

Ray Kroc
Ernest Hemingway
Katharine Hepburn
Jackson Pollock
Eleanor Roosevelt
Franklin D. Roosevelt

THE TEN TOP CELEBRITIES OF THE DECADE

The editors of *People* magazine picked ten people who "dominated the decade" in some way, the decade meaning 1974-1984, *People's* first ten years in publication. Here are the ten winners:

1974—Richard M. Nixon

"Washed out by Watergate"—"He was reelected in one of the most overwhelming landslides in American history. He conducted the last successful foreign policy this nation has known... Why did he bungle a presidency that held so much promise? Why has he never said he is sorry?"

1975—Patty Hearst

"From bank robber to suburban housewife"—"The unwitting symbol of a terrorist cause became a conservative—and a contented mom."

1976—Farrah Fawcett

"A new kind of love goddess"—"An all-American angel soared as a new kind of TV sex symbol, but she soon found her wings clipped."

1977—John Travolta

"He found Astaire-way to stardom"—"The national pulse was thumping to the disco beat and, as Tony Manero in *Saturday Night Fever*, Travolta embodied that phenomenon with sass and panache."

1978—Louise Brown

"The miracle child of science"—"The world's first 'test-tube baby' ushered in a revolution in fertility ... The first human conceived outside of a mother's body."

149

1979—Ayatollah Ruhollah Khomeini

"Ungodly acts from a man of God"—"He brought terror and fear to his land and ours—and all in the name of Allah. . . . He was the blood enemy of the Shah, he held the United States hostage for 15 months."

1980—John Lennon

"Pioneer of a generation's rite of passage"—"Like his vibrant life and art, his tragic death shook a generation and marked the tumult of the times. . . . Lennon was more than a rock 'n' roll hero. His life and music mirrored—even foreshadowed—the bittersweet experiences of a watershed generation whose youth seemed history when his voice was silenced."

1981—Princess Diana

"She smiled and a fairy tale came to life"—"The sudden metamorphosis from teacher at the Young England Kindergarten in London's Pimlico district to the world's most prominent princess."

1982—Jane Fonda

"Working out reshaped her image"—"Ricocheting from Hollywood brat to sex siren . . . to warrior maiden . . . Perhaps Fonda's most astonishing incarnation has been her latest: aerobics ambassador."

1983—Ronald Reagan

"Leadership and luck overrode his setbacks"—"At 73, our oldest President retains the strength of the idealogue and the suppleness of a Great Communicator. It is a formidable combination. . . . He's America's man on horseback."

MEN AND WOMEN OF THE YEAR

(According to the Hasty Pudding Institute of 1770)

The Hasty Pudding Institute of 1770, the oldest dramatic club in the United States, is a club composed of Harvard University students active in dramatic arts. A Woman of the Year Award has been given annually by the club since 1951 "to the performer who has made a lasting and impressive contribution to the world of entertainment." The Man of the Year Award was established in 1967. Here are the winners:

WOMAN OF THE YEAR		MAN OF THE YEAR
1951	Gertrude Lawrence	—
1952	Barbara Bel Geddes	—
1953	Mamie Eisenhower	—
1954	Shirley Booth	—
1955	Debbie Reynolds	—
1956	Peggy Ann Garner	—
1957	Carroll Baker	—
1958	Katharine Hepburn	—
1959	Joanne Woodward	—
1960	Carol Lawrence	—
1961	Jane Fonda	—
1962	Piper Laurie	—
1963	Shirley MacLaine	—
1964	Rosalind Russell	—
1965	Lee Remick	—
1966	Ethel Merman	—
1967	Lauren Bacall	Bob Hope
1968	Angela Lansbury	Paul Newman
1969	Carol Burnett	Bill Cosby
1970	Dionne Warwick	Robert Redford
1971	Carol Channing	James Stewart
1972	Ruby Keeler	Dustin Hoffman
1973	Liza Minnelli	Jack Lemmon
1974	Faye Dunaway	Peter Falk
1975	Valerie Harper	Warren Beatty
1976	Bette Midler	Robert Blake
1977	Elizabeth Taylor	Johnny Carson
1978	Beverly Sills	Richard Dreyfuss
1979	Candice Bergen	Robert DeNiro
1980	Meryl Streep	Alan Alda
1981	Mary Tyler Moore	John Travolta
1982	Ella Fitzgerald	James Cagney
1983	Julie Andrews	Steven Spielberg
1984	Joan Rivers	Sean Connery
1985	Cher	Bill Murray

THE MOST BORING PEOPLE
(AND EVENTS) OF 1984

(according to the Boring Institute, Maplewood, N.J.)

The 1984 presidential election
George Burns
Bo Derek
Bob Hope
Michael Jackson
Michael Landon
Prince Charles and Princess Diana
Andy Rooney
George Shultz
Frank Sinatra
Sharlene Wells (Miss America)

THE WORLD'S MOST LOVABLE NERDS

International Bachelor Women, an organization based in Los Angeles, California, recently announced its list of "The World's Most Lovable Nerds." Here is the list:

Woody Allen
Howard Cosell
Pee Wee Herman
John McEnroe
Ed McMahon
Walter Mondale
Prince Charles
Michael Reagan
Ronald Reagan, Jr.
Orville Redenbacher
Andy Rooney

THE TEN MOST ROMANTIC COMPOSERS

The 2,000 members of the Lonely Hearts' Club of America recently voted on the most popular pop composers whom they considered the "most romantic." As Jane Holland, president of the Lonely Hearts, said: "We feel the love inspired by these particular songwriters has been most responsible for a decline in our membership. Here are those romantic composers:

Air Supply	Paul McCartney
Paul Anka	Melissa Manchester
Boy George	Barry Manilow
The Everly Brothers	Lionel Richie
John Lennon	Toni Tennille

PEOPLE WHO GAVE AWAY $1 MILLION OR MORE IN 1984

Mrs. Hazel Ruby McQuain: $8,000,000 to West Virginia University

Arthur J. Decio: $6,200,000 to the University of Notre Dame

Temple Hoyne Buell: $5,000,000 to Columbia University

John W. Berry: $5,000,000 to Dartmouth College

Henry J. Knott: $5,000,000 to Mount Saint Mary's College

Cary M. Maguire: $5,000,000 to Southern Methodist University

Norton Simon: Two residences valued at $4,600,000 to UCLA

William F. Farley: $3,500,000 to Bowdoin College

Louise M. Davies: $3,000,000 to the San Francisco Symphony

Sam P. Harn family: $3,000,000 to the University of Florida Foundation

Charles W. and Margre Henningson Durham: $3,000,000 to Iowa State University

Ambassador and Mrs. Maxwell Gluck: $3,000,000 to the University of Kentucky

Malcolm Forbes: $3,000,000 to Princeton University

Thomas J. Bannan: $2,300,000 to the University of Santa Barbara

Robert S. and Margaret Folsom: $2,250,000 to Southern Methodist University

Phillip A. Rhodes: Pritchards Island, valued at $2,200,000 to the University of South Carolina

R. David Thomas: $2,100,000 to Ohio State University Cancer Research Institute

Mrs. Eleanor Houston Smith: land valued at $2,000,000 to the University of Maine

James A. Michener: $2,000,000 to Swarthmore College

Lineberger family: $2,000,000 to the University of North Carolina

Michael C. Carlos: $1,750,000 to Emory University

Holland Ware: $1,500,000 to Emory University

Fred Kuehne: $1,500,000 to Washburn University of Topeka

A. Guy Crouch: land valued at $1,400,000 to Baylor University

David H. and Carol Feinberg: $1,300,000 to Princeton University

Dr. and Mrs. George N. Boone: $1,250,000 to the University of Southern California School of Dentistry

Rev. Andrew M. Greeley: $1,250,000 to the University of Chicago

Bernard J. Lasker: $1,250,000 to Mount Sinai Medical Center

Stone family: $1,250,000 to the University of Wisconsin

Roy R. Neuberger: $1,200,000 to the State University of New York (Purchase)

Ostrom Enders: ornithological volumes valued at $1,200,000 to Trinity College

Mrs. Sarah George: $1,000,000 to Alleghany College

John C. Whitehead: $1,000,000 to the Boy Scouts of America

William P. Clements: $1,000,000 to the Boy Scouts of America

Jerome L. Greene: $1,000,000 to Columbia School of Law

John and Janice Fisher: $1,000,000 to DePauw University

Mrs. Reunette Harris: $1,000,000 to Emory University

Rev. Nicholas J. Langenfeld's family: $1,000,000 to Fordham University

Mr. and Mrs. Robert Daugherty: $1,000,000 to Hastings College

Mitchell Wolfson, Jr.: $1,000,000 to Princeton University

Herbert Banden-Brul: $1,000,000 to Rochester Memorial Art Gallery

Jack and Laura Lee Blanton family: $1,000,000 to Southern Methodist University

Ryoichi Sasakawa: $1,000,000 to UCLA

Dorothy and Leonard Straus: $1,000,000 to UCLA School of Medicine

Frank W. Clark, Jr.: $1,000,000 to UCLA

Richard J. Franke: $1,000,000 to Yale University

Lucy Goldschmidt Moses: $1,000,000 to Yale University

FRIARS CLUB CELEBRITIES

The Friars Club is an outgrowth of the Press Agents' Association, which was established in 1904 to eliminate the fraudulent acquisition of free passes to New York theaters. The club changed through the years and now has become a refuge largely for show business people (performers and behind-the-scenes people) and a sponsor of annual luncheons and dinners to honor esteemed members. Essentially, the objectives of the club are "to foster and promote the best professional and fraternal relations among all its members" and "to foster and promote better understanding between persons engaged in the theatrical profession or any other branch of the amusement field or related fields."

Many comedians, of course, belong to the Friars Club, but Groucho Marx, curiously, was never a member, suggesting that he was a man of his word. He didn't want to join any club that would have him as a member.

Here is a list of the Friars Club officers, most of whom are familiar names, and also two lists of those celebrities who have been honored at their annual dinners and "roasted" at their annual luncheons. (The roasts, by the way, are not related to the Dean Martin roasts occasionally seen on television.)

FRIARS CLUB OFFICERS

Joey Adams, Biographer
Paul Anka, Herald
Gene Baylos, Knight
Milton Berle, Abbot Emeritus
George N. Burns, Proctor
Red Buttons, Scribe Emeritus
Sammy Cahn, Lyricist
Johnny Carson, Prior
Howard Cosell, Historian
Sammy Davis, Jr., Bard
Jack L. Green, Scribe
Tom Jones, Knight
Alan King, Monitor
Norman King, Samaritan
Jack H. Klein, Treasurer
Robert Merrill, Monk
Dr. S. L. Meylackson, Treasurer Emeritus

Alexander Rose, Sergeant at Arms
Frank Sinatra, Abbot
David W. Tebet, Director of Special Events
William B. Williams, Dean
Henny Youngman, Squire

FRIARS ANNUAL TESTIMONIAL DINNER HONOREES

1950   Joe E. Lewis
1951   Jack Benny
1952   "Friars Frolic"
1953   Bob Hope
1954   George Jessel
1955   Dean Martin and Jerry Lewis
1956   Ed Sullivan
1957   Perry Como
1958   Mike Todd
1959   Steve Allen
1960   Dinah Shore
1961   Garry Moore
1962   Joe E. Lewis
1963   Milton Berle
1964   Joey Bishop
1965   Johnny Carson
1966   Sammy Davis, Jr.
1967   Steve Lawrence and Eydie Gorme
1968   Ed Sullivan
1969   Barbra Streisand
1970   Tom Jones
1971   Alan King
1972   Jack Benny and George Burns
1973   Carol Burnett
1974   Don Rickles
1975   Walter Matthau and George Burns (the Sunshine Boys)
1976   Frank Sinatra
1977   Kirk Douglas
1978   David Brinkley Walter Cronkite, and Howard K. Smith
1979   Johnny Carson

1980 Dean Buddy Howe and Dr. Henry Kissinger
1981 Burt Reynolds and Buddy Hackett
1982 Cary Grant
1983 Elizabeth Taylor
1984 William B. Williams and Dean Martin

FRIARS CELEBRITY LUNCHEON HONOREES

1950 Sam Levenson
1951 Phil Silvers, Harry Delf, and Mel Allen
1952 Leo Durocher, Rocky Marciano
1953 Sophie Tucker, Milton Berle, and Eddie Fisher
1954 Red Buttons and Martha Raye
1955 Humphrey Bogart
1956 Sammy Davis, Jr.
1957 Joe E. Lewis and Red Buttons
1958 Joe E. Lewis and Red Buttons
1959 Milton Berle, Jimmy Cannon, and Jack E. Leonard
1960 George Burns and Joey Bishop
1961 Lucille Ball and Alan King
1962 Jan Murray and Johnny Carson
1963 Steve Lawrence and Jack Benny
1964 Jack Carter, Nat King Cole, and Sammy Davis, Jr.
1965 Soupy Sales, Marty Allen, and Steve Rossi
1966 Al Kelly and Mayor John V. Lindsay
1967 Milton Berle
1968 Earl Wilson, Harry Belafonte and Don Rickles
1969 Jack E. Leonard
1970 David Frost
1971 Phil Silvers and Pat Henry
1972 Ed McMahon
1973 Henny Youngman and Howard Cosell
1974 George Raft and Milton Berle
1975 Redd Foxx
1976 Telly Savalas and Joey Adams
1977 Tom Jones and Totie Fields
1978 Neil Simon
1979 Robert Merrill and Norm Crosby
1980 George Steinbrenner and Pat Henry
1981 Jim Dale
1982 Dick Shawn
1983 Sid Caesar
1984 Roger Grimsby, Chuck Scarborough and Rolland Smith

J. FRED MUGGS AWARD WINNERS

J. Fred Muggs was just an average chimpanzee waiting on tables in New York's theater district until he was discovered by an agent and selected to appear on television's "Today" show with Dave Garroway. J. Fred always mugged the camera, and the public went ape but he rarely made a monkey of himself. *TV Guide* now gives out J. Fred Muggs awards every year for "those who excelled at making monkeys of themselves." IIere are a few winners of their 1984 awards:

"The Andy Rooney Curmudgeon of the Year Award"
This award did not go to Cleveland Amory but to Andy Rooney of "60 Minutes" who "walked out in the middle of his speech to the Alaska Press Club because he objected to the presence of a local TV news crew taping his remarks." Now he knows what it's like to be invaded by Mike Wallace, a cameraman, and a microphone.

"OK, Liz, but You Have to Return the Ashtrays and Towels"
For appearing in *one* episode of "Hotel," actress Elizabeth Taylor was paid $100,000 and eleven designer outfits especially made for her in the show.

"You Think Dat's Bad, Judge, You Shoulda Seen His Acting on 'Taxi'"
When former boxer, turned-actor Tony Danza ("Taxi") was convicted of assaulting a security guard at a Manhattan restaurant, the judge told Danza and his cohort, "You acted as buffoons."

"Only Nosey Female Interviewers, Fool"
Barbara Walters, "ABC's intrepid questioner," asked "The A-Team's" Mr. T if he had ever killed anybody.

"What Technique, What Finesse, What a Fine Player He Is!"
In the Stockholm Open tennis matches, America's badboy John McEnroe was shown "calling the Swedish umpire a jerk, ... hitting a ball into the stands, ... swatting a soft-drink can, ... [and] getting smacked in turn with a $21,000 fine and a 21-day suspension for his antics." McEnroe should have a great second career in professional wrestling if he can put on a few pounds.

"First They Hiss Him, Then They Miss Him"
"After years of bemoaning Howard Cosell's commentary in the broadcast booth, sportswriters and TV critics last fall bemoaned the departure" of Howard Cosell from ABC's "Monday Night Football."

CELEBRITY "CLOWNS" OF 1984

Larry Harmon, better known as Bozo the Clown, announced the following winners of his 1984 "Bozo Awards":

Showbiz—Prince, for his "less-than-royal" behavior on stage and off.
Politics—Gary Hart, for his preoccupation with the word "new."
Newsmaker—Elizabeth Taylor, for giving new meaning to the word "hospital-ity."
Funster—Vanessa Williams, for giving the Miss America proceedings a new theme song, "There she goes, without any clothes, Miss America . . ."
Journalism—Andy Rooney, for single-handedly inventing a new and profitable industry, "nagcasting."
Sports—A tie between Carl Lewis and John McEnroe, for their Academy Award-worthy portrayals of the quintessential "spoilsport." (Bozo says that these two athletes have their egos insured with Lloyds of London.)
Honorable Mention—John DeLorean, for super-salesmanship.

YOUNGEST AND OLDEST OSCAR WINNERS

Youngest Best Supporting Actress	Tatum O'Neal (age 10)
Youngest Best Supporting Actor	Timothy Hutton (age 19)
Youngest Best Actress	Janet Gaynor (age 22)
Youngest Best Actor	Richard Dreyfuss (age 29)
Oldest Best Actress	Katharine Hepburn (age 74)
Oldest Best Actor	Henry Fonda (age 76)
Oldest Best Supporting Actor	George Burns (age 80)
Oldest Best Supporting Actress	Peggy Ashcroft (77)

ACTORS AND ACTRESSES WHO HAVE WON MORE THAN ONE OSCAR

ACTOR	NUMBER OF OSCARS
Walter Brennan	3
Marlon Brando	2
Gary Cooper	2
Robert De Niro	2
Melvyn Douglas	2
Jack Lemmon	2
Fredric March	2
Jack Nicholson	2
Anthony Quinn	2
Jason Robards	2
James Stewart	2
Spencer Tracy	2
Peter Ustinov	2

ACTRESS	
Katharine Hepburn	4
Ingrid Bergman	3
Bette Davis	2
Olivia de Havilland	2
Sally Field	2
Jane Fonda	2
Helen Hayes	2
Glenda Jackson	2
Vivien Leigh	2
Luise Rainer	2
Maggie Smith	2
Meryl Streep	2
Elizabeth Taylor	2
Shelley Winters	2

GREAT ACTORS WHO NEVER WON AN OSCAR

ACTOR	NO. OF OSCAR NOMINATIONS
Richard Burton	7
Peter O'Toole	7
Paul Newman	5
Charles Boyer	4
Montgomery Clift	4
Claude Rains	4
Kirk Douglas	3
William Powell	3
Charlie Chaplin	2
James Dean	2
John Garfield	2
Cary Grant	2
Edward G. Robinson	0

Note: Charles Boyer won a special award in 1942; Cary Grant won a special award in 1969; Charlie Chaplin won his special award in 1971; and Edward G. Robinson won a special award in 1972.

GREAT ACTRESSES WHO NEVER WON AN OSCAR

ACTRESS	NO. OF OSCAR NOMINATIONS
Deborah Kerr	6
Geraldine Page	6
Thelma Ritter	6
Rosalind Russell	5
Agnes Moorehead	4
Barbara Stanwyck	4
Greta Garbo	3
Gloria Swanson	3
Ruth Chatterton	2
Judy Garland	2
Liv Ullman	2
Marlene Dietrich	1

Note: Judy Garland won a special Oscar in 1939; Greta Garbo won an honorary Oscar in 1954.

ACTORS NOMINATED FOR BEST ACTING AND BEST SUPPORTING ROLES IN THE SAME YEAR

NOMINATIONS

Fay Bainter (1938)	Best Actress for *White Banners*
	Best Supporting Actress* for *Jezebel*
Teresa Wright (1942)	Best Actress for *Pride of the Yankees*
	Best Supporting Actress* for *Mrs. Miniver*
Barry Fitzgerald (1944)	Best Actor and Best Supporting Actor* for *Going My Way*
Jessica Lange (1982)	Best Actress for *Frances*
	Best Supporting Actress* for *Tootsie*

* Won the Oscar—a double nomination seems to guarantee a Best Supporting role award.

THE NO-SHOW MUST GO ON: THE 32ND EMMY AWARDS

On Sunday, September 7, 1980, the 32nd annual Emmy Awards ceremony was held, but few performers showed up. Because of an actors' strike they were boycotting the show. Here are some of the people who didn't show up and some who did:

NO-SHOWS	SHOWED UP
Ed Asner	Steve Allen
Barbara Bel Geddes	Barbi Benton
Johnny Carson	Powers Boothe (the actor who played
Cathryn Damon	Rev. Jim Jones in "The Guyana
Michael Landon	Tragedy")
Nancy Marchand	Dick Clark
Stuart Margolin	David Copperfield
Harry Morgan	Jayne Kennedy
Richard Mulligan	Dick Smothers
Bob Newhart	Tom Smothers
Lee Remick	Jim Stafford
Loretta Swit	

THE KENNEDY CENTER HONOREES

In 1978 the Kennedy Center for the Performing Arts in Washington, D.C., created its Honors awards to acknowledge the achievements of five distinguished contributors to the performing arts. The following are the recipients for the first seven years:

1978

Marian Anderson (contralto)
Fred Astaire (dancer-actor)
George Balanchine (choreographer)
Richard Rodgers (Broadway composer)
Artur Rubinstein (pianist)

1979

Aaron Copland (composer)
Ella Fitzgerald (jazz singer)
Henry Fonda (actor)
Martha Graham (dancer-choreographer)
Tennessee Williams (playwright)

1980

Leonard Bernstein (composer-conductor)
James Cagney (actor)
Agnes de Mille (choreographer)
Lynn Fontanne (actress)
Leontyne Price (soprano)

1981

Count Basie (jazz composer-pianist)
Cary Grant (actor)
Helen Hayes (actress)
Jerome Robbins (choreographer)
Rudolf Serkin (pianist)

1982

George Abbott (Broadway producer)
Lillian Gish (actress)
Benny Goodman (jazz clarinetist)
Gene Kelly (dancer-actor)
Eugene Ormandy (conductor)

1983

Katherine Dunham (dancer-choreographer)
Elia Kazan (director-author)
Frank Sinatra (singer)
James Stewart (actor)
Virgil Thomson (music critic-composer)

1984

Lena Horne (singer)
Danny Kaye (entertainer)
Gian Carlo Menotti (composer)
Arthur Miller (playwright)
Isaac Stern (violinist)

THE MOST POPULAR AND LEAST POPULAR CELEBRITIES

Marketing Evaluationst/TVQ Inc., based in Port Washington, N.Y., evaluates celebrities every year in terms of their likeability (or lack of it) and familiarity. The familiarity score is the percent of people who are familiar with the celebrity, the Q-score is the percent of people familiar with the celebrity who like the celebrity, and the negative Q-score is the percent of people who know of the celebrity and don't like the person. Here are the people's choices, the good and the bad:

The Most Popular Comedians and Comediennes

	RATING "ONE OF MY FAVORITES"	TOTAL FAMILIAR	POSITIVE Q RATING
Carol Burnett	41%	90%	45%
Bob Hope	38%	91%	42%
George Burns	36%	90%	40%
Bill Cosby	34%	91%	37%
Lucille Ball	34%	95%	36%
Eddie Murphy	20%	51%	39%

The Least Popular Comedians and Comediennes

	RATING "FAIR" OR "POOR"	TOTAL FAMILIAR	NEGATIVE Q RATING
Don Rickles	34%	85%	40%
David Letterman	29%	61%	40%
Dick Martin	29%	72%	47%
Buddy Hackett	28%	78%	36%
Norm Crosby	24%	62%	39%

The Most Popular Sports Personalities

	RATING "ONE OF MY FAVORITES"	TOTAL FAMILIAR	POSITIVE Q RATING
Sugar Ray Leonard	19%	82%	23%
Dorothy Hamill	17%	81%	21%
Tom Landry	16%	60%	27%
Steve Garvey	14%	60%	23%
Magic Johnson	14%	58%	24%

165

The Least Popular Sports Personalities

	RATING "FAIR" OR "POOR"	TOTAL FAMILIAR	NEGATIVE Q RATING
Muhammed Ali	51%	91%	56%
Billie Jean King	38%	79%	48%
Joe Namath	32%	83%	39%
John McEnroe	29%	64%	45%
Cathy Rigby	26%	73%	36%

The Most Popular Newscasters

	RATING "ONE OF MY FAVORITES"	TOTAL FAMILIAR	POSITIVE Q RATING
Walter Cronkite	29%	85%	34%
Dan Rather	23%	80%	29%
Harry Reasoner	22%	77%	29%
Paul Harvey	21%	66%	32%
David Brinkley	19%	81%	23%

The Least Popular Newscasters

	RATING "FAIR" OR "POOR"	TOTAL FAMILIAR	NEGATIVE Q RATING
Barbara Walters	31%	79%	39%
Jack Anderson	16%	53%	30%
Hodding Carter	11%	37%	30%
Morton Dean	11%	53%	21%

The Most Popular Sports Announcers

	RATING "ONE OF MY FAVORITES"	TOTAL FAMILIAR	POSITIVE Q RATING
Merlin Olsen	21%	71%	30%
Terry Bradshaw	14%	73%	19%
Don Meredith	14%	77%	18%
Roger Staubach	13%	69%	19%
Bryant Gumbel	12%	54%	22%

The Least Popular Sports Announcers

	RATING "FAIR" OR "POOR"	TOTAL FAMILIAR	NEGATIVE Q RATING
Howard Cosell	57%	82%	70%
Bruce Jenner	28%	70%	40%
Jimmy "The Greek" Snyder	28%	56%	50%
Fran Tarkenton	25%	78%	32%
O. J. Simpson	24%	79%	30%

RADIO PERSONALITIES: THE TOP SPOT RADIO PERSONALITIES IN THE U.S. BY SHARE OF AUDIENCE*

PERSONALITIES	CALL LETTERS/CITY	SHARE OF AUDIENCE
Bob Steele	WTIC/Hartford	35.9%
Don Cole, Kent Pavelka, and Walt Kavanaugh	KFAB/Omaha	31.7%
Bob Sievers	WOWO/Ft. Wayne	30.6%
Jorge Guilleen, Hugo De La Cruz	KGBT/McAllen-Brownsville	30.4%
Bill Hickok	WIIC/Bridgeport	29.6%
Charlie Boone, Roger Erickson	WCCO/Minneapolis	29.4%
Bob Hardy, Bill Wilkerson	KMOX/St. Louis	29.3%
Luther Massingill	WDEF/Chattanooga	25.5%
Alden Aaroe	WRVA/Richmond	25.1%
Wayne Gardner, Bill Jones and Tim O'Neil	WKSJ/Mobile	25.0%
Bob Krahling	WHBC/Canton	24.7%
Gary Todd	WIBC/Indianapolis	23.8%
Kim Kahoana	KSSK/Honolulu	23.5%
John Cigna	KDKA/Pittsburgh	23.4%
Andy Rent	WCUZ/Grand Rapids	22.5%
Randy Rice, Jim Nasium	WFMF/Baton Rouge	22.5%
Gordon Light	WXBO/Bristol	21.9%
Claude Tomlinson	WIVK-FM/Knoxville	21.5%
Maury O'Dell	WPTF/Raleigh-Durham	21.3%
Jeff "J.J." Jackson	WKSJ/Mobile	21.3%

*Percent of the total radio listening audience in that area who are tuned to that particular show.

Source: *Radio & Records* magazine

RADIO PERSONALITIES: THE TOP SPOT
RADIO PERSONALITIES IN THE U.S.
BY AUDIENCE SIZE

PERSONALITIES	CALL LETTERS/CITY	AUDIENCE SIZE
Paul Smith, Michael O'Neil, and Jim McGiffert	WINS/New York	1,781,500
Shadow Stevens	WHTZ/New York	1,389,300
Jim Donnelly, Robert Vaughn	WCBS/New York	1,332,600
Scott Shannon, Ross Brittain	WHTZ/New York	1,200,000
Rick Dees	KIIS/Los Angeles	1,091,500
Pat St. John	WPLJ/New York	1,047,700
Jim Kerr	WPLJ/New York	1,016,700
John Gambling	WOR/New York	1,013,400
Don Imus	WNBC/New York	1,009,700
Wally Phillips	WGN/Chicago	952,100
Larry Lujack	WLS/Chicago	921,100
Chip Hobart	WAPP/New York	915,200
Ron O'Brien	KIIS/Los Angeles	913,300
Charlie Burger, Mary Thomas	WRKS/New York	900,600
Stan Burns, Dave Henderson	WINS/New York	855,000
Ken Webb	WRKS/New York	838,200
Paco	WKTU/New York	824,900
Dick Shepherd	WPAT/New York	804,400
Dan Daniel	WYNY/New York	786,700
Jay Thomas	WKTU/New York	779,200

Source: *Radio & Records* magazine

THE TEN BEST-SELLING SINGERS AND GROUPS OF 1984

The following are the singers and groups who sold the most record albums in 1984, according to *Billboard* magazine:

Culture Club (Epic) "Colour by Numbers"
Duran, Duran (Capitol) "Seven and the Ragged Tiger"
Footloose soundtrack (Columbia)
Michael Jackson (Epic) "Thriller"
Billy Joel (Columbia) "An Innocent Man"
Huey Lewis and The News (Chrysalis) "Sports"
ZZ Top (Warner Bros.) "Eliminator"
Lionel Richie (Motown) "Can't Slow Down"
Van Halen (Warner Bros.) "1984"
The Police (A&M) "Synchronicity"

Source: *Billboard*, November 1, 1983–November 17, 1984

THE FIFTEEN CELEBRITIES WHO HAVE APPEARED ON THE COVER OF *PEOPLE* MAGAZINE AT LEAST FIVE TIMES

	NO. OF TIMES ON *PEOPLE* COVERS
Elizabeth Taylor	8
John Travolta	8
Cher	7
Princess Diana	7
Farrah Fawcett	7
Olivia Newton-John	7
Jackie Kennedy Onassis	7
Jane Fonda	6
John Ritter	6
Princess Caroline	5
Paul Newman	5
Dolly Parton	5
Brooke Shields	5
Sylvester Stallone	5
Barbra Streisand	5

Source: *People* magazine, 1974-1984

THE BEST AND WORST SELLING MAGAZINE COVERS OF 1984

(or How Michael Jackson Helped Magazine Sales!)

MAGAZINE	BEST SELLER	WORST SELLER
Time	Michael Jackson (March 19, 1984)	Walter Mondale (June 18, 1984)
Newsweek	"Taxbusters" (December 10, 1984)	Boy George (January 23, 1984)
Rolling Stone	Michael Jackson (March 15, 1984)	Steve Martin (November 8, 1984)
People	Michael Jackson (February 13, 1984) 10th Anniversary issue (March 5, 1984)	Child Stars (November 12, 1984)
Life	Year-end issue (January 1984)	Father of quintuplets (July 1984)
Sports Illustrated	Swimsuit issue (February 13, 1984)	Soviet Olympic boycott (May 21, 1984)

WAXING FAMOUS: CELEBS AT MADAME TUSSAUD'S

One true sign of being a real celebrity is getting one's likeness immortalized in wax and exhibited at Madame Tussaud's wax museum in London, England. The following contemporaries have their wax figures and physiognomies at the museum:

Prince Andrew	Nastassia Kinski
Bjorn Borg	John McEnroe
David Bowie	Charles Manson and "The Family"
Boy George	Liza Minnelli
Barbara Cartland	Francois Mitterand
Prince Charles	Dolly Parton
Constantine Chernenko	Pele
Princess Diana	Prince Phillip
Queen Elizabeth II	Andre Previn
Ella Fitzgerald	Muammar Al Qadaffi
Larry Hagman	Ronald Reagan
David Hockney	Telly Savalas
King Hussein of Jordan	Margaret Thatcher
Glenda Jackson	Lech Walesa
Michael Jackson	Andrew Lloyd Webber
Pope John Paul II	

SPACE CELEBRITIES: THE FIRST TEN MEN IN SPACE

Yuri Gagarin (USSR) April 12, 1961
Alan B. Shepard (U.S.A.) May 5, 1961
Virgil I. Grissom (U.S.A.) July 21, 1961
G. S. Titov (USSR) August 6, 1961
John H. Glenn (U.S.A.) February 20, 1962
Malcolm Scott Carpenter (U.S.A.) May 24, 1962
Andrian Grigorievich Nikolayev (USSR) August 11, 1962
Pavel Romanovich Popovich (USSR) August 12, 1962
Walter M. Schirra (U.S.A.) October 3, 1962
Leroy Gordon Cooper (U.S.A.) May 15, 1963

CELEBRITY JAILBIRDS

The following well-known people have spent at least one night in jail. Tabloids often distort the amount of time these celebs were behind bars but what else is new. For example, many people think that singer Johnny Cash has spent a lot of time in some prison when, in fact, he has spent about seven nights in local jails for relatively minor offenses like possession of amphetamines. Here are the celebrity jailbirds:

Brendan Behan	Martin Luther King, Jr.
Chuck Berry	Sophia Loren
Truman Capote	Malcolm X
Johnny Cash	Robert Mitchum
Tony Danza	Nick Nolte
Freddie Fender	Griffin O'Neal
Mahatma Gandhi	Ryan O'Neal
Harry Golden	Duncan Renaldo
Richard Harris	O.J. Simpson
O. Henry	Bill Tilden
Howard Hesseman	Mae West
Stacy Keach	Oscar Wilde
	Dave Winfield

CELEBRITIES WHO MAKE THE BEST COPY FOR GOSSIP COLUMNISTS ACCORDING TO LIZ SMITH

Liz Smith, generally acknowledged to be the best gossip columnist in the U.S., turns out engaging copy about the famous and presumably rich every day—their comings and comings-out, their goings, their partying, their dining, and the like. Here are the people who made the best copy for Miss Smith and her colleagues during the past year:

Warren Beatty	The Reagans
Boy George	Burt Reynolds
Princess Caroline	Frank Sinatra
Joan Collins	Princess Stephanie
Princess Diana	Barbra Streisand
Cyndi Lauper	Elizabeth Taylor
Jackie Onassis	Tina Turner
Prince	

What They Do With Themselves 13.

CELEBRITY HOBBIES

Kareem Abdul-Jabbar	conga drums
Alan Alda	chess
Woody Allen	clarinet, jazz
Julie Andrews	yoga, skiing
Alan Arkin	guitar
Edward Asner	collects shells
Lucille Ball	backgammon
Johnny Bench	bowling, golf, bridge
Peter Benchley	scuba diving, tennis, skiing
Michael Bennett	skiing
George Benson	guitar, motorcycles, sports cars
Candice Bergen	photography
Jacqueline Bisset	cooking, ping-pong, antiques
Robert Blake	motorcycling
Debby Boone	cooking
Jeff Bridges	carpentry, gardening
Tom Brokaw	backpacking, jogging
William F. Buckley, Jr.	sailing, harpsichord
Carol Burnett	yoga
James Caan	karate, judo, steer roping
Michael Caine	cooking, antiques
Glen Campbell	golf, tennis
David Carradine	race car driving
Keith Carradine	backpacking
Diahann Carroll	cooking
Johnny Carson	astronomy, tennis, drums, flying
Dick Cavett	collects Indian arrowheads and artifacts
Julia Child	piano
Jill Clayburgh	cooking

CELEBRITY HOBBIES, continued

James Coburn	flute
Tim Conway	golf, furniture refinishing
Walter Cronkite	sailing
Jim Dale	puppets, antique clowns and toys
John Davidson	horseback riding, sailing, backpacking
Sammy Davis, Jr.	golf
John Denver	skiing, hiking, gardening (in the nude!)
Bo Derek	horseback riding, weightlifting
Bruce Dern	jogging
Neil Diamond	chess, motorcycling, fencing
Peter Duchin	fly fishing
Clint Eastwood	jogging, tennis, golf
Blake Edwards	judo, yoga
Julie Nixon Eisenhower	needlepoint
Werner Erhard	sailing
Julius Erving	tennis, golf, chess
Peter Falk	pool
Mia Farrow	sewing, patchwork quiltmaking, yoga
Farrah Fawcett	skiing, hunting, fishing, sculpture
Sally Field	piano, quiltmaking, sewing
Carrie Fisher	cooking, antiques
Roberta Flack	piano, pinball playing
Harrison Ford	carpentry
Greta Garbo	walking
James Garner	race car driving
Phyllis George	piano, tennis
Paul Michael Glaser	motorcycling, guitar
Elliott Gould	cardplaying
Cary Grant	tennis, swimming, horseback riding
Merv Griffin	tennis, raising quarterhorses
Larry Hagman	Zen meditation
Mark Hamill	baking cakes, Monopoly
Deborah Harry	yoga
David Hartman	golf, tennis, baseball
Goldie Hawn	knitting, sewing, cooking
Hugh M. Hefner	backgammon
Margaux Hemingway	skiing, horseback riding, fishing
Audrey Hepburn	skiing
Katharine Hepburn	bicycling
Charlton Heston	tennis

176

Dustin Hoffman	collects toy clowns
Bob Hope	golf
Anthony Hopkins	astronomy, piano
Rock Hudson	chess, astronomy, crossword puzzles
John Huston	hunting, gambling
Lauren Hutton	knitting, safaris
Kate Jackson	skiing, tennis
Reggie Jackson	collects automóbiles
Mick Jagger	African art
Billy Joel	boxing
Gabe Kaplan	poker
Edward Kennedy	swimming, sailing
James J. Kilpatrick	stamp collecting, bridge, flags
Jack Klugman	gambling on and raising horses
Ted Knight	antiques, L. A. Dodgers
Steve Lawrence	tennis
Jack Lemmon	piano
G. Gordon Liddy	piano, singing German lieder
Hal Linden	saxophone
Rich Little	pool, trivia
Sophia Loren	poker, cooking
George Lucas	reading comic books
Paul McCartney	reading science fiction and comic books
Lee Majors	hunting
Dean Martin	golf
Lee Marvin	sailing
Johnny Mathis	sports, cooking
Ed McMahon	boating, photography
Edwin Meese	collects model squad cars and statuettes of pigs
Toshiro Mifune	sailing, fishing, hunting, flying
Robert Mitchum	horseback riding
Anne Murray	golf
Jim Nabors	opera
Joe Namath	golf, fishing
Bob Newhart	golf
Paul Newman	race car driving
Wayne Newton	raising Arabian horses, antique cars
Mike Nichols	raising Arabian horses
Jack Nicholson	skiing
Richard M. Nixon	piano, baseball, bowling
Ted Nugent	archery, hunting

CELEBRITY HOBBIES, continued

Jackie Onassis	horseback riding
Donny Osmond	skiing, skating
Marie Osmond	skiing, skating
Gregory Peck	tennis, gardening
Anthony Perkins	bicycling, jogging
Prince Charles	polo, sailing, cello
Tony Randall	opera, ballet, trivia
Dan Rather	tennis, jogging, hunting, fishing
Lou Rawls	tennis, golf, Ping-Pong
Ronald Reagan	horseback riding
Robert Redford	tennis, skiing, horseback riding
Christopher Reeve	skiing, tennis, flying
Lee Remick	embroidery
Burt Reynolds	collecting art
John Ritter	racquetball, collects Beatle records
Joan Rivers	needlepoint
Cliff Robertson	tennis, skiing, golf, flying
Smokey Robinson	golf, jogging, yoga
Kenny Rogers	golf, tennis, poker, photography, sailing
Roy Rogers	bowling, raising horses
Diana Ross	tennis, skiing
Morley Safer	baking pies and cakes
Charles Schulz	tennis, hockey, golf
George C. Scott	chess
Tom Selleck	volleyball
Gene Shalit	bassoon, puns
Omar Sharif	bridge
Brooke Shields	collects autographs and stuffed animals, horseback riding
Dinah Shore	golf, tennis, needlepoint, cooking
Neil Simon	tennis
O.J. Simpson	jogging, tennis, poker
Jaclyn Smith	water skiing, horseback riding
Tom Snyder	collecting teddy bears and other toy animals, antique trains
Suzanne Somers	gourmet cooking, poetry
Stephen Sondheim	word games, anagrams
David Soul	baseball, songwriting
Sissy Spacek	tap dancing, backpacking
Mickey Spillane	skindiving, fishing

MacLean Stephenson	golf, fishing
Rod Stewart	soccer
Donald Sutherland	jogging
Cheryl Tiegs	tennis
Peter Ustinov	tennis, oenology, Havana cigars
John Travolta	flying, cars
Robert Wagner	tennis, skiing, sailing, flying
Mike Wallace	tennis
Orson Welles	magic
Paul Williams	race car driving
Robin Williams	jogging, yoga, backgammon
Dave Winfield	photography
Henry Winkler	rock gardening
Jonathan Winters	American Indian lore
Joanne Woodward	cooking, needlepoint

CELEBRITY POLO PLAYERS

Polo is not your run-of-the-mill sport. Polo fields are not quite as common as bowling alleys or tennis courts and not everyone can afford to buy a couple of special Argentinian-bred horses and stable them in Greenwich, Connecticut, or on the island of Jamaica. And not everyone can ride a horse!

Originally played in Persia, polo eventually spread to India where British soldiers took up the sport and imported it to England in 1871. Soon thereafter it was played in America. British prime minister Winston Churchill played polo during his military service in India. General George Patton, Will Rogers, and Theodore Roosevelt were also polo enthusiasts. The following are some contemporary polo players from the celebrity world and their handicaps:*

	HANDICAP
Michael Butler (producer)	1
Wilt Chamberlain (basketball player)	(not rated)
Prince Charles of England (royalty)	4
Alex Cord (actor)	1
William Devane (actor)	-1
Tom Holland (sculptor)	1
Tommy Lee Jones (actor)	2
Stacy Keach (actor)	-1
Jerzy Kosinski (author)	(not known)
Stefanie Powers (actress)	0
Taki (writer)	2

*Unlike a golfer, the higher a polo player's handicap the better he is. A player with a handicap of 9 or above, for example, is in the top 1% of the sport.

CELEBRITY GOLFERS

Glen Campbell (8 handicap)
Perry Como (6 handicap)
Mike Douglas (Jack Nicklaus said that Douglas
  played like a pro!)
James Garner (4 handicap)
Mickey Mantle (3 handicap)
Johnny Mathis (9 handicap)
Joe Namath (shoots in the 80's)
Smokey Robinson (12 handicap)

CELEBRITY ARTISTS

The following people are well known but not for their artistic talents. However, they are excellent artists.

Xavier Cugat
Gunter Grass
Rocky Graziano
Charlton Heston
Jack Lord
Robert Redford
Morley Safer (paints hotel rooms)
Red Skelton (paints clowns)
John Updike
Billy Dee Williams
Jonathan Winters (surrealist, of course!)

Politics 14.

FAMOUS AMERICAN WRITERS WHO RAN FOR POLITICAL OFFICE

Jimmy Breslin
A political cohort of Norman Mailer in 1969, columnist Breslin ran for city council president and lost, although he did attract more votes than Mailer did.

William F. Buckley, Jr.
The writer and editor ran as the Conservative candidate in the New York City mayoralty race in 1965 and lost to fellow Yale graduate John Lindsay.

Jack London
A dedicated Socialist, London ran for the office of mayor in Oakland, California, in 1905. Receiving only a few hundred votes, he lost.

Norman Mailer
The outspoken author tried to get the Democratic nomination in the New York City mayoralty race in 1969. With a Maileresque campaign slogan ("No more bullshit!"), he finished fourth out of five candidates.

James Michener
The noted author ran for Congress as a Democrat in the Bucks County, Pennsylvania, district in 1962. He lost.

Upton Sinclair
Like Jack London, Sinclair was also a Socialist with political aspirations. As a Socialist, he ran for Congress twice, governor of California once, and the U.S. Senate once, losing every time. In 1934

he ran for the governorship again, this time as a Democrat, and still lost.

Hunter S. Thompson

The "gonzo" journalist ran for sheriff of Pitkin County, Colorado, (where Aspen is located) in 1970. His radical platform stirred up interest, but he lost to the incumbent Democrat.

Gore Vidal

In 1960 Vidal ran on the Democratic ticket for a congressional seat in upstate New York. He lost but did receive more votes in the district than John F. Kennedy received.

ACTORS WHO BECAME POLITICIANS

Ronald Reagan is not the first actor to run for office, nor will he be the last. Watch out for Charlton Heston, Jane Fonda, Robert Redford, and a few others. In the interim here are some thespians-turned-politicians:

Rex Bell	Elected lieutenant governor of Nevada in 1954.
Shirley Temple Black	Ran for Congress in 1967 but lost to Paul McCloskey; appointed a delegate to the UN's 24th General Assembly, 1969-1970; appointed U.S. ambassador to Ghana in 1974-1976.
Wendell Corey	Elected to the Santa Monica City Council in 1965, he sought the Republican nomination for California 28th congressional district seat in 1966, but lost to incumbent Alonzo Bell.
Helen Gahagan Douglas	Elected congresswoman from California's 14th district in the 1940s; ran for U.S. Senate in 1950 but lost to Richard M. Nixon.

Charlie Farrell	Mayor of Palm Springs, California, for seven years.
Al Jolson	Elected mayor of Encino, California in 1937.
Jack Kelly	Elected mayor of Huntington Beach, California, in 1983
John Davis Lodge	Governor of Connecticut in the early 1950s; ambassador to Spain, 1955-1961; ambassador to Argentina, 1969-1973.
George Murphy	U.S. senator from California, 1964-1979; he lost his reelection bid to John Tunney.

CELEBRITY POLITICS

DEMOCRATS

Edward Asner
Kay Ballard
Warren Beatty
Ellen Burstyn
Carol Channing
Bill Cosby
Colleen Dewhurst
Neil Diamond
Michael Douglas
Linda Evans
Morgan Fairchild
Sally Field
Jane Fonda
Margot Kidder
Robert Klein
Norman Lear
Hal Linden
Shirley MacLaine
Paul Newman
Randy Newman
Tony Randall
Robert Redford
Donald Sutherland

REPUBLICANS

June Allyson
Ray Bolger
Pat Boone
Chuck Connors
Mike Connors
Robert Conrad
Jimmy Dean
Clint Eastwood
Buddy Ebsen
Dale Evans
Chad Everett
Eva Gabor
Helen Hayes
Charlton Heston
Bob Hope
Dorothy Lamour
Fred MacMurray
Dean Martin
Wayne Newton
Donald O'Connor
Roy Rogers
Cesar Romero
Jill St. John

CELEBRITY POLITICS, continued

DEMOCRATS

James Taylor
Marlo Thomas
Lily Tomlin
Andy Williams
Shelley Winters
and a cast
   of thousands . . .

REPUBLICANS

Tom Selleck
Frank Sinatra
Robert Stack
Jimmy Stewart
Robert Wagner
Clint Walker
Jonathan Winters
Loretta Young
Efrem Zimbalist, Jr.
and a cast
   of hundreds . . .

WOMEN IN THE U.S. HOUSE AND SENATE

The first U.S. congresswoman was Jeannette Rankin, a Republican elected from Montana. She served from 1917 to 1919 and from 1941 to 1943. The first female U.S. senator was Rebecca Latimer Felton, a Democrat from Georgia, who was appointed by the governor of Georgia in 1922 to fill the vacancy created by the death of Thomas Edward Watson. Women haven't exactly come a long way but they're working at it. Here is a list of the women in the 1985 U.S. House and Senate, representing 4.5% of the total representatives and senators:

WOMEN IN THE SENATE

Florida: Paula Hawkins (R)
Kansas: Nancy Kassebaum (R)

WOMEN IN THE HOUSE OF REPRESENTATIVES

California: Barbara Boxer (D); Sala Burton (D);
          Bobbi Fiedler (R)
Colorado: Patricia Schroeder (D)
Connecticut: Nancy Johnson (R); Barbara Kennelly (D)
Illinois: Cardiss Collins (D); Lynn Martin (R)
Kansas: Jan Meyers (R)
Louisiana: Corinne "Lindy" Boggs (D)

186

Maine: Olympia Snowe (R)
Maryland: Helen Bentley (R); Beverly Byron (D);
    Marjorie Holt (R); Barbara Mikulski (D)
Nebraska: Virginia Smith (R)
Nevada: Barbara Vucanovich (R)
New Jersey: Marge Roukema (R)
Ohio: Marcy Kaptur (D); Mary Rose Oakar (D)
Rhode Island: Claudine Schneider (R)
Tennessee: Marilyn Lloyd (D)

Source: National Women's Political Caucus

THE TWENTY MOST INFLUENTIAL PEOPLE
OUTSIDE GOVERNMENT

According to a *U.S. News & World Report* survey, the following
twenty Americans are the most influential people outside government (in rank order):

Roone Arledge (president of ABC-TV news and sports)
Cardinal Joseph Bernadin (archbishop of Chicago)
Jerry Falwell (head of the Moral Majority)
Milton Friedman (economist)
Billy Graham (evangelist)
Katharine Graham (publisher of the *Washington Post*
    and *Newsweek*)
Lee Iacocca (chairman of Chrysler)
Jesse Jackson (civil rights leader and presidential candidate)
Michael Jackson (entertainer)
Lane Kirkland (head of AFL-CIO)
Henry Kissinger (former Secretary of State)
Ted Koppel (ABC-TV commentator)
Ralph Nader (consumer advocate)
Dan Rather (CBS-TV anchorman)
David Rockefeller (ex-chairman of Chase Manhattan)
Roger B. Smith (chairman of General Motors)
Arthur Sulzberger (publisher of *The New York Times*)
Ted Turner (communications entrepreneur)
Walter Wriston (chairman of Citicorp)

Source: *U.S. News & World Report*, May 14, 1984

NIXON'S OFFICIAL ENEMIES LIST

When White House counsel John Dean submitted the Nixon presidency "enemies list" to the Senate Watergate Committee on June 27, 1973, here are the names that appeared:

Alexander E. Barkan, AFL-CIO Committee on Political Education
John Conyers, Michigan congressman
Maxwell Dane, Doyle Dane Bernbach advertising agency
Sid Davidoff, aide to Mayor John Lindsay of New York
Ronald Dellums, California congressman
S. Harrison Dogole, Globe Security System
Charles Dyson, Dyson-Kissner Corporation
Bernard T. Feld, Council for a Livable World
Ed Guthman, *Los Angeles Times*
Morton Halprin, Common Cause
Samuel M. Lambert, National Education Association
Allard Lowenstein, New York congressman
Mary McGrory, Washington newspaper columnist
Stewart Rawlings Mott, General Motors heir and philanthropist
S. Sterling Munro, Jr., congressional aide
Paul Newman, movie actor
Arnold M. Picker, United Artists Corporation
Daniel Schorr, CBS News correspondent
Howard Stein, Dreyfus Corporation
Leonard Woodcock, United Auto Workers

MORE NIXON "ENEMIES"

The following people were not on Nixon's "official" enemies list but they were not exactly his favorites:

Bella Abzug, New York congresswoman
Sherman Adams, aide to President Eisenhower
Stewart Alsop. political columnist
Julie Andrews, actress
Polly Bergen, actress
Jimmy Breslin, newspaper columnist
James Brown, singer
Willie Brown, California assemblyman
Patrick Caddell, political pollster
Godfrey Cambridge, comedian

Mortimer Caplin, former head of IRS
Clark Clifford, former secretary of defense
Paul Conrad, *Los Angeles Times* political cartoonist
Charles Diggs, former Michigan congressman
Richard Dougherty, campaign press secretary for Senator
    McGovern
Angier Biddle Duke, former U.S. chief of protocol
Frederick G. Dutton, University of California regent
Max Factor, cosmetics entrepreneur
Frances "Sissy" Farenthold, Texas politician
John Kenneth Galbraith, economist and former ambassador to
    India
James M. Gavin, lieutenant general, U.S. Army
Ralph Gleason, *San Francisco Chronicle* jazz critic
Charles Goodell, former New York senator (and Republican)
Ernest Gruening, former senator from Alaska
Gene Hackman, movie actor
Gary Hart, senator from Colorado
Hugh M. Hefner, publisher of *Playboy* magazine
Aaron Henry, civil rights activist from Mississippi
Kareem Abdul-Jabbar, professional basketball player
Jesse Jackson, civil rights activist
Henry Kimelman, fund raiser and finance chairman for Senator
    McGovern,
Coretta Scott King, widow of Dr. Martin Luther King, Jr.
Gilman Kraft, brother of columnist Joseph Kraft
Burt Lancaster, movie actor
Norman Lear, TV producer
John Lindsay, former mayor of New York City
Shirley MacLaine, movie actress
Norman Mailer, author
Frank Mankiewicz, campaign director of Senator McGovern
Howard M. Metzenbaum, senator from Ohio
Lawrence O'Brien, national chairman of Democratic party
Max Palevsky, industrialist
Linus Pauling, Nobel Prize-winning chemist
William Proxmire, senator from Wisconsin
Tony Randall, movie actor
Joseph Robbie and wife, owners of the Miami Dolphins
Pierre Salinger, former press secretary to John F. Kennedy
Connie Stevens, singer and actress
Elizabeth Taylor, movie actress

George Wald, Harvard professor
Paul C. Warnke, SALT talks negotiator
Harold Willens, organizer of Businessmen Against the War
Joanne Woodward, movie actress

Sources: David Wise's *The American Police State; The Los Angeles Times*, December 21, 1973; and the Tax Reform Research Group/ABC News.

HUAC'S CELEBRITY ENEMIES LIST

The following well-known people were among those mentioned "unfavorably" in testimony before the House Un-American Activities Committee (HUAC), as reported in *The New Republic* in the early 1950s:

Leonard Bernstein	Norman Mailer
Pearl Buck	Reinhold Niebuhr
Erskine Caldwell	Dorothy Parker
Clarence Darrow	Arthur Schlesinger
Albert Einstein	Budd Schulberg
George Gershwin	Upton Sinclair
Ernest Hemingway	Frank Lloyd Wright

NINE CELEBRATED LAWYERS–THE U.S. SUPREME COURT JUSTICES

Ask most *honest* lawyers what they'd *really* like to be and they'll usually reply, "A Supreme Court justice." Even the public likes Supreme Court justices; they rank high on popularity polls. Appointed by the president of the United States and confirmed by the U.S. Senate, here are the most celebrated lawyers in the country:

JUSTICE	YEAR BORN	RELIGION	APPOINTED BY:
Harry A. Blackmun	1908	Methodist	Nixon
William J. Brennan, Jr.	1906	Roman Catholic	Eisenhower
Warren E. Burger	1907	Presbyterian	Nixon

190

Thurgood Marshall	1908	Episcopalian	Johnson
Sandra Day O'Connor	1930	Episcopalian	Reagan
Lewis F. Powell, Jr.	1907	Presbyterian	Nixon
William H. Rehnquist	1924	Lutheran	Nixon
John Paul Stevens, III	1920	Protestant	Ford
Byron R. White	1917	Episcopalian	Kennedy

U.S. PRESIDENTS WHO SERVED
LESS THAN FOUR YEARS IN OFFICE

PRESIDENT	TIME IN OFFICE
Chester Arthur	3 yrs. 166 days
Millard Fillmore	2 yrs. 236 days
Gerald Ford	2 yrs. 150 days
James Garfield	199 days
Warren G. Harding	2 yrs. 151 days
William H. Harrison	32 days
Andrew Jackson	3 yrs. 322 days
John F. Kennedy	2 yrs. 306 days
Zachary Taylor	1 yr. 128 days
John Tyler	3 yrs. 332 days

RONALD REAGAN'S PRESIDENTIAL
MEDAL OF FREEDOM RECIPIENTS

The Presidential Medal of Freedom was established in 1963 by President John F. Kennedy to expand presidential recognition of meritorious service, which had been granted as the Medal of Freedom since 1945. The following people have been given the award since President Ronald Reagan has been in office:

RECIPIENT	YEAR AWARDED
Howard H. Baker, Jr. (government service)	1984
George Balanchine (choreographer)	1983
Count Basie (jazz pianist)	1985
James H. (Eubie) Blake (composer-pianist)	1981
Paul W. (Bear) Bryant (football coach)	1983*

RONALD REAGAN'S PRESIDENTIAL MEDAL
OF FREEDOM RECIPIENTS, continued

RECIPIENT	YEAR AWARDED
James Burnham (editor-historian)	1983
James Francis Cagney (actor)	1984
Whittaker Chambers (public servant)	1984*
James Cheek (educator)	1983
Leo Cherne (economist-humanitarian)	1984
Terence Cardinal Cooke (theologian)	1984*
Denton Arthur Cooley, M.D. (heart surgeon)	1984
Jacques-Yves Cousteau (undersea explorer)	1985
Tennessee Ernie Ford (singer)	1984
R. Buckminster Fuller (architect-geometrician)	1983
Hector P. Garcia, M.D. (humanitarian)	1984
Gen. Andrew J. Goodpaster (soldier-diplomat)	1984
Rev. Billy Graham (evangelist)	1983
Ella T. Grasso (Connecticut governor)	1981*
Philip C. Habib (diplomat)	1982
Bryce N. Harlow (government service)	1981
Eric Hoffer (philosopher-longshoreman)	1983
Jerome Holland (civil rights leader)	1985
Sidney Hook (philosopher)	1985
Jacob K. Javits (government service)	1983
Walter H. Judd (government service)	1981
Jean J. Kirkpatrick (former ambassador to U.N.)	1985
Lincoln Kirstein (ballet director)	1984
Louis L'Amour (author)	1984
Morris L. Leibman (lawyer)	1981
George Low (NASA administrator)	1985
Clare Booth Luce (author-diplomat)	1983
Dumas Malone (historian)	1983
Mabel Mercer (jazz singer)	1983
Norman Vincent Peale (theologian)	1984
Simon Ramo (industrialist)	1983
Frank Reynolds (TV journalist)	1985
S. Dillion Ripley (conservationist)	1985
Gen. Carlos P. Romulo (Philippino statesman)	1984
Jack Roosevelt Robinson (baseball player)	1984*
Mohammed Anwar El-Sadat (statesman)	1984*
Eunice Kennedy Shriver (humanitarian)	1984
Frank Sinatra (singer and actor)	1985

James Stewart (actor)	1985
Kate Smith (singer)	1982
Mother Teresa (missionary)	1985
Charles B. Thornton (industrialist)	1981
Gen. Albert Coady Wedemeyer (soldier)	1985
Gen. Charles Yeager (test pilot)	1985

*awarded posthumously

FOURTEEN FAMOUS EX-CIA AND OSS AGENTS

The Office of Strategic Services (OSS) was the U.S. intelligence branch during World War II and the forerunner of the Central Intelligence Agency. Here are some well-known people who served in either the OSS or CIA:

Stewart Alsop (OSS)—Political columnist
Tom Braden (OSS)—Political columnist and TV talk show co-host
William F. Buckley, Jr. (CIA)—Political columnist, editor, author
Michael Burke (OSS)—Ex-president of Madison Square Garden
George Bush (OSS)—U.S. Vice president
Julia Child (OSS)—Author/cook
Allen Dulles, Richard Helms, William Colby, and George Bush, all
    OSS veterans, became directors of the CIA
Arthur Goldberg (OSS)—Supreme Court justice
Herbert Marcuse (OSS)—Political theorist
Walt Rostow (OSS)—L.B.J.'s national security advisor
William Sloane Coffin (CIA)—Chaplain
Arthur Schlesinger (OSS)—Historian

*Richard Cummings' book *The Pied Piper* (Grove Press, 1985) alleges that the late Congressman Allard K. Lowenstein, civil-rights and antiwar activist, had a working relationship with the CIA for many years. The allegation has been strongly denied by family friends and counsel, and by Frank C. Carlucci, a former CIA deputy director.

The Tube

CELEBRITIES' FAVORITE TV SHOWS

Members of the Screen Actors Guild were recently asked to list their favorite TV shows of all time. Here's the top ten list:

"I Love Lucy"
"The Dick Van Dyke Show"
"The Mary Tyler Moore Show"
"The Honeymooners"
"M*A*S*H"

"Cheers"
"Leave It to Beaver"
"The Twilight Zone"
"Hill Street Blues"
"Gunsmoke"

AMERICA'S FAVORITE TV SHOWS

The sorts of shows the stars like themselves are pretty well matched by the kinds of programs that are most popular in America's 83.3 million television-owning households. In one recent month A. C. Nielsen provided this list of the top ten network programs:

"ABC Sunday Night Movie"
"Dallas"
"60 Minutes"
"A-Team"
"Simon & Simon"

"Falcon Crest"
"Magnum, P.I."
"Dynasty"
"Hotel"
"AfterMash"

GUESTS ON THE FIRST AND LAST BROADCASTS OF "THE ED SULLIVAN SHOW"

"The Ed Sullivan Show" (originally "The Toast of the Town") was on the air for twenty-three years, an impressive run. As comedian Alan King observed, "Ed does nothing but he does it better than anyone else on television." Here are the people who appeared on the first and last broadcasts of Sullivan's show:

FIRST BROADCAST (JUNE 20, 1948)

Ruby Goldstein (fight referee)
Lee Goodman and Jim Kirkwood (comedy team)
John Kokoman (singing fireman)
Kathryn Lee (ballerina)
Monica Lewis (singer)
Eugene List (pianist)
Dean Martin and Jerry Lewis (comedy team)
Richard Rodgers and Oscar Hammerstein II
    (composer, lyricist)

LAST BROADCAST (JUNE 6, 1971)

Carol Channing (comedienne)
Topo Gigio (puppet act)
Pat Henry (comedian)
Robert Klein (comedian)
Gladys Knight and the Pips (singing group)
Peter Nero (pianist)
Jerry Vale (singer)
Caterina Valente (singer)

The Grim Reaper 16.

SHOT AND LIVED

James Arness (war wound)
Art Carney (war wound)
Robert Dole (war wound)
Blake Edwards (war wound)
Peter Fonda (suicide attempt)
James Garner (war wound)
Uri Geller (war wound)
Pope John Paul II (assassination attempt)
Lee Marvin (war wound)
Jennifer O'Neill (accident)
Jack Palance (war wound)
Joe Pepitone (childhood accident)
Ronald Reagan (assassination attempt)
Nelson Rockefeller (childhood accident)
George Wallace (assassination attempt)

WELL-KNOWN PEOPLE WHO DIED OUTSIDE THE UNITED STATES

	PLACE OF DEATH
Sherwood Anderson	Panama
Larry Blyden	Morocco
Richard Burton	Switzerland
Charlie Chaplin	Switzerland
Bing Crosby	Spain
Bernard Fall	Vietnam
Marty Feldman	Mexico City
Sonja Henie	While flying from Paris, France, to Oslo, Norway

197

WELL-KNOWN PEOPLE WHO DIED OUTSIDE THE UNITED STATES, continued

PLACE OF DEATH

Howard Hughes	In a plane flying from Acapulco to Houston, Texas
Paul Lukas	Morocco
Steve McQueen	Mexico
Gordon Parks, Jr.	Kenya
Tyrone Power	Spain
Gregory Ratoff	Switzerland
Eddie Rickenbacker	Switzerland

FAME (INFAMY) BY ASSASSINATION

ASSASSIN	VICTIM (INTENDED VICTIM)
Mehmet Ali Agca	Pope John Paul II
Arthur Herman Bremer	George Wallace
Mark David Chapman	John Lennon
John W. Hinckley, Jr.	Ronald Reagan
Sarah Jane Moore	Gerald R. Ford
Lee Harvey Oswald	John F. Kennedy
James Earl Ray	Dr. Martin Luther King, Jr.
Sirhan Bishara Sirhan	Robert F. Kennedy

WELL-KNOWN PEOPLE WHOSE RELATIVES DIED IN NAZI PRISON CAMPS

RELATIVE(S)

Menachem Begin	mother and father
Robert Clary	mother and father and ten other relatives
Milos Forman	mother and father
Audrey Hepburn	an uncle and cousin
Marcel Marceau	father
Roman Polanski	mother
Simon Wiesenthal	89 relatives

WELL-KNOWN PEOPLE WHO KILLED
ANOTHER PERSON

Movie director **John Huston** admitted running over and killing a
child while driving a car.

Actor **Paul Kelly** was imprisoned for manslaughter after killing
another actor during a brawl.

Singer **Claudine Longet** shot and killed skier Spider Sabich.

Actor **Basil Rathbone** shot and killed a German soldier at close
range in World War I.

Opera singer **Lawrence Tibbett** accidentally stabbed another
singer during a performance; the performer later died.

CELEBRITIES WHOSE PARENTS
COMMITTED SUICIDE

Truman Capote's mother
Jane Fonda's mother
Mariette Hartley's father
Josh Logan's father

Walker Percy's father
Elizabeth Swados's mother
Ted Turner's father

LIVED TO A RIPE OLD AGE

When people told Groucho Marx that he was a sexagenarian he was extremely flattered, perhaps for the wrong reasons. When he was told that he was an octogenarian, he began to feel that he was getting old. He was, but lived until age 86, which is longer than the span Providence grants most people. Here are some well-known people who became not only sexagenarians, but who lived to at least Groucho's age:

	AGE AT DEATH
Adolph Zukor	103
Grandma Moses	101
Father Divine	100
John Nance Garner	98
John D. Rockefeller	98
George Bernard Shaw	94
Lila Acheson Wallace	94
Donald Crisp	93
Somerset Maugham	92
Sunny Jim Fitzsimmons	91
Samuel Goldwyn	91
William Powell	91
Konrad Adenaur	90
Winston Churchill	90
Herbert Hoover	90
Joan Miro	90
Alfred P. Sloan	90
Gilbert Anderson (Bronco Billy)	89
Brooks Atkinson	89
Mary Baker Eddy	89
Bronco Billy Anderson	88
William Randolph Hearst	88
Gen. Mark W. Clark	87
Jane Darwell	87
Groucho Marx	86
Mary Pickford	86
Walter Pidgeon	86

Index